Close to the Land

The Way We Lived in North Carolina, 1820–1870

Manufactured in the United States
of America

*Library of Congress Cataloging in
Publication Data*

Clayton, Thomas H. (Thomas Hale),
1949–
    Close to the land.

    Bibliography: p.
    1. North Carolina—History—1775–
1865.   2. North Carolina—Social life
and custom.   3. Historic sites—North
Carolina—Guide-books.   4. North
Carolina—Description and travel—1981–
—Guide-books.   I. Nathans, Sydney.
II. North Carolina. Dept. of Cultural
Resources.   III. Title.
F258.C6 1983   975.6′03   82-20143
ISBN 0-8078-1551-9
ISBN 0-8078-4103-X (pbk.)

Close to the Land

The Way We Lived in North Carolina, 1820–1870

Published for the North Carolina Department of Cultural Resources

by The University of North Carolina Press   *Chapel Hill*

Editor:
Sydney Nathans

Consultants:
Larry Misenheimer
William S. Price, Jr.

This publication has been made possible through a grant from the National Endowment for the Humanities.

The Way We Lived series was developed under the guidance of the Historic Sites Section, Division of Archives and History, North Carolina Department of Cultural Resources.

(Title page) Outbuilding at Mordecai Historic Park, Raleigh, Wake County.

(Right) Barn at Pioneer Farmstead, Swain County.

Christine Alexander took the photographs not otherwise credited in this book.

Text by Thomas H. Clayton

Research and Marginalia by Jean B. Anderson

Design and Art Editing by Christine Alexander

Experiencing History

This series of books, *The Way We Lived*, is based on the premise that the past can be most fully comprehended through the combined impact of two experiences: reading history and visiting historic places. The text of this volume (the third in a series of five) is therefore coordinated with a variety of historical sites. Most places pictured as well as those mentioned in the margins are open to the public regularly or by appointment. Information about visiting and exact locations may be obtained locally.

Our objective in specifying sites has not been to compile a complete or comprehensive catalogue of historic places in the state; rather it has been to guide the reader to a representative selection of sites that exemplify the major themes of the text.

Many excellent examples that might have served our purpose equally well have been omitted. Others now in the planning or working stages of restoration may be expected to swell the number of unnamed sites. We can only leave to the readers the pleasure of their discovery and the hope that this volume will serve as a stimulus to further reading and exploration.

Contents

Settlers on the move.

Overview

Victorian America

It was the Victorian Age. Born in 1819, Victoria ascended the throne of England in her teens and in 1870 was still queen. Her reign remained constant in a half-century that was otherwise tumultuous with change. New words suggested the altering dimensions of thought and the material world: technology, industrialist, engineer, journalism, individualism, booster, sodbuster, saloon and Sunday school. Most life had been lived at a walking pace in the century before. New inventions from this period accelerated the tempo of life and linked remote parts of the country and the globe: the railroad, the telegraph, the steamship, the reaper, the sewing machine, the transatlantic cable.

In the American portion of the Victorian world, the United States was first and foremost a young republic. One of every three persons was under ten. Over half the population was under thirty. The population grew so fast—doubling in size every twenty-five years—that if the pace had continued, today we would be a nation of one billion.

Young people were not only numerous; they were restless. The restlessness and ambition of youth were fueled by the explosion of opportunities for adventure and advancement. New land provided an enormous boon to this generation. The American portion of the continent had doubled in 1803 with the Louisiana Purchase. Near mid-century it doubled again, and the United States became a continental nation, with the acquisition of Texas, Oregon, and the massive southwestern territory wrested from Mexico in 1848.

Treaties and war made the expansion of the agricultural frontier possible; canals, railroads, steel plows, and the reaper made western settlement and farming profitable. Long before gold was discovered in California in 1848, young men and women were leaving the East behind. As many as one of every four persons born in the seaboard states and New England swarmed inland in search of new opportunities, with the aspiring from the Carolinas journeying to the southwestern lands of Alabama and Mississippi as well as Indiana and Illinois in the Old Northwest.

But the energy and optimism of the Republic in this half-century came not only from the westward surge. The era was one of unprecedented growth of towns and cities, industry and commerce. By 1860 New York City had its first million inhabitants. The populations of other coastal and inland cities doubled and redoubled. One day in

Chicago in the mid-1830s, lots that sold for $150 in the morning sold for $5,000 by nightfall. Even small towns throbbed with business, as blacksmiths and merchants, artisans and lawyers, set up shop and rang up profits. While few factories in the modern sense existed, the hum of cottage industry became a din of manufacturing. With power provided by rivers and then steam-driven machines, with labor supplied first by young New England women and then by immigrant families, textile manufacturing led the way. In 1820 eight of ten Americans had made their living on the farm. By 1870 over half of those employed worked in pursuits outside of agriculture.

The furious expansion of commerce and industry was made possible by breakthroughs in transportation. Creation of an ambitious network of canals followed the dazzling success of the Erie Canal in 1825 and linked coastal cities with the interior. In the 1830s the steamboat made the Mississippi the nation's great inland waterway. Dwarfing and dominating the canal system from the 1840s onward was the railroad. By 1860 the railroads of the nation had laid thirty thousand miles of track and had attracted a billion dollars of investment. In 1869 the Golden Spike commemorated the linking of New York and California by a transcontinental railway.

Little wonder, then, that much of the era from 1820 to 1870 was characterized by buoyant optimism. A continent possessed, space conquered by locomotives, productivity multiplied by mechanization: what boundaries had not or could not be broken? Leading political figures of the era—Andrew Jackson, Abraham Lincoln, Ulysses

Locomotive. Raleigh and Gaston Railroad. N.C. State Archives.

Grant—had risen from poverty or obscurity to the presidency. They were stunning symbols of an America in motion, of a society of self-made men.

The creativity of the period was not confined to business or politics or to men alone. It was also an age of remarkable social experiment. The inspiration for much social innovation was anxiety: would the rush of the young to the frontier and the city create a nation of rootless and profiteering vagrants? Thousands turned their energy into the effort to reform and reinforce the moral character of Americans. Public schools forged good character, Sunday schools implanted virtue, YMCAs gave Christian shelter to restless youth. Victorian Americans pioneered in the creation of penitentiaries, insane asylums, and reform schools, each designed to reclaim and reform those driven to crime or insanity by the temptations or insecurities of commercial life. Social innovation extended even to the Victorian family. The family was asked to become a refuge of affection in a world of turbulence and amorality. Women especially, as mothers and teachers, were called on to domesticate the passions and uplift the sensibilities of men competing for place and fortune.

Perhaps it is not surprising that a society immense in its creative energies would also be colossal in its contradictions. A slave society existed and grew amidst a free one. The mechanization that enhanced productivity for many, degraded the skills and made hireling laborers of others. The benefits of communications with distant markets were matched by the risks of ties to the national economy, which reliably collapsed every twenty years. Women who joined the movement to free slave families discovered their own bonds, and initiated their own movement, when men sought to silence female speakers at antislavery forums. Indeed, breaking from bondage became a motif for many by mid-century, and the American vocabulary of 1870 reflected the struggles undertaken to resolve Victorian tensions. "Woman's rights" and "free love," strike and socialism, emancipation and Reconstruction—what a different world it was from that of fifty years before!

The Tar Heel State

A traveler visiting North Carolina in 1820 would immediately have noticed that all things visible seemed to be agricultural. The dwellings that dotted the landscape—plantations and slave quarters, frame houses and log cabins, gristmills and weatherboard churches—all were country places. The pace of people at work was decidedly rural. From sunup to sundown, most worked hard but without great hurry. Play was intermixed with work, rather than reserved until day was done. Frequent drams of liquor lubricated the day's labor; songs

Flailing wheat.

accompanied toil in the fields; a barn raising was a mixture of boister-ousness and brawn. If the visitor looked closely, he would also have detected a paradox. Few who farmed did farming only. If a small farmer wanted a wagon, he made it. Whiskey? He distilled his own. The same multiplicity of talents was evident in slave communities, where blacks were preachers and trappers, midwives and home-gardeners, as well as tillers in a master's field.

The visitor would eventually have found towns and townspeople too, of course. Carolinians from the countryside and village came to town to trade and sell at the marketplace, to talk politics and do legal battle at the county courthouse. Town residents supported skilled furniture-makers and able school-mistresses, who provided cosmopolitan amenities for a cultivated society. Yet even town physicians and lawyers, ministers and bankers doubled, or at least dabbled, in agriculture. For the overwhelming majority of North Carolinians in 1820, agriculture was the main business of life and shaped decisively the way they lived.

If the same traveler had returned to North Carolina in 1860, he might well have recorded contradictory impressions in his letters home. Signs of change abounded. Almost a thousand miles of rail-roads laced the state linking east and west. North Carolina's notori-ous illiteracy, circumscribing the mental horizons of the majority in 1820, was now under attack in the twenty-five hundred common schools that brought a few months' learning each year to a hundred thousand of the young. The dozen newspapers of 1820 had become seventy-five in 1860, a handful of hamlets had grown to flourishing small towns, and modest water-powered textile mills had established the outposts of a factory frontier in the state.

Yet what might have struck the traveler most about the forty years between 1820 and 1860 were not the signs of change but the strength of continuities. The great planters had expanded in number and diversified their crops to include inland cotton as well as leaf tobacco. But as a class this elite remained small, its lands the best, its influence large. In 1860 as in 1820, a third of North Carolinians were black and most were enslaved. Still predominant were the mass of yeomen farmers and their families, cultivating small farms with methods and tools familiar to their grandfathers. If making money and a life of elegance were the ambitions of the planters, and making both possible was the duty of the blacks, to "make do" remained the goal and self-sufficiency the ultimate accomplishment of most small farmers.

The persistence of simple self-sufficiency and tradition in farm-ing and daily life might well have troubled the traveler in 1860. For much of the rest of the nation had taken a different course in the nineteenth century. Outside the South, cities and factory towns, machines and improved transportation had changed the pace of life.

4

On the farm, in villages as well as cities, a spirit of enterprise had taken hold. The market economy had spread everywhere, and both single people and families moved frequently in search of the best opportunities of "Commerce, Commerce, Commerce!" To outsiders who traveled through North Carolina and to many natives as well, the Tar Heel state—by doing most things as it had always done them—had fallen behind.

Yet, for all its traditionalism, North Carolina was not a stagnant society. The Tar Heel of legend, content to live lazily off the fat of the land, a bit of a brawler, proud that his mind was unpolluted by book learning, suspicious of higher culture as effeminate and alien, was more myth than reality. Curiosity, resourcefulness, and invention abounded, but they occurred within the boundaries of a rural world. Those boundaries frequently were narrow, often limited to the locality where a North Carolinian had grown up. Yet that small world was known with matchless intimacy. Footpaths and streams, soil and climate, neighbor and kin—these were the objects of curiosity and passion, loyalty and legend, struggle and mastery. Family was central, and a true map of North Carolina would record not only the roads and streams and farms and churches, but also the connections of kin. It was a countryside of cousins. Clans of cousins formed family alliances and intricate networks of mutual aid. It was a folk society, personal and passionate, ambitious and enterprising in its own terms.

The terms of life were altered by 1870. Not only did emancipation change the relationship between black and white, planter and freedman. The Civil War expanded horizons and shook old premises. Over a hundred thousand North Carolinians had left their localities, traveled hundreds of miles from home, and seen a wider part of the world. Women had managed farms and plantations while their men were away. Though most returned to rebuild after the war, deprivation created new opportunities. More and more farmers would plant crops for market. Others were ready to go beyond the plow and the plantation to take their chances with factories and the life of commerce. Ambitions and forces for change, channeled and contained for fifty years within the bounds of plantation life, slave communities, and local enterprise, were unleashed. The next half-century would be dramatically different from the last.

Sydney Nathans

Farms with dwellings like the Pioneer Farmstead, on the Oconaluftee River, Swain County, in the Great Smoky Mountains National Park, made survival possible for independent and isolated pioneers.

Many outbuildings, among them barn, crib, pigpen, chicken house, springhouse, and blacksmith shop, were vital for self-sufficient farmers to "make do or do without" in the wilderness.

The frame farmhouse near Fremont, Wayne County, where Governor Charles B. Aycock was born is a typical middleclass home of the period.

Rural Community

Provincial and conservative, the people of the "Rip Van Winkle" state were invariably characterized by outside observers, such as Frederick Law Olmsted, as well deserving their proverbial reputation for "ignorance and torpidity." Overwhelmingly rural, North Carolinians were isolated from the world around them, as well as each other, by geographical barriers, limited means of transportation, and their own independent spirit. However "backward" and "indolent," most Tar Heels had a more discerning, if not more favorable, view of their lifestyle and themselves. Times were hard; there is no doubt. Days were long and rewards were slight. Yet an increasing number of Carolinians had succeeded in purchasing their own farms. And, as the *Fayetteville Observer* in 1837 proudly pointed out: "The great mass of our population is composed of people who cultivate their own soil, owe no debt, and live within their means. It is true we have no overgrown fortunes, but it is also true that we have few beggars."

Beyond pride in personal accomplishment, nineteenth-century Carolinians, regardless of economic means or social status, were sustained by an unequivocal commitment to family life and a strong sense of local community. Young and old alike met in the hundreds of rural churches which dotted the landscape to share in a common religious experience and the animated conversation that invariably followed the sermon. The essential economic goods and services provided by the country store or nearby mill were complemented by its social function as a public forum for the lively discussion of any and every topic from tomorrow's weather to today's politics. And the growing number of academies and schools served to heighten the community's esteem as well as prepare its younger members to meet the challenges of the outside world.

Yet undoubtedly the most important bond among those who composed the rural community was their common interest in cultivating the land. Agriculture was their way of life, and it informed their every thought and action. The farm, whether ten acres or ten thousand, was the basic unit of economic production and social organization. It was there that the vast majority of Carolinians could be found—working their fields, preparing their meals, rearing their children, and living out their lives.

7

Mordecai House, Mordecai Historic Park, Raleigh, Wake County. The Greek Revival addition to Henry Lane's colonial cottage made an antebellum plantation house for the Moses Mordecai family.

Plantation Life

In North Carolina the "Old South" of fiction and film did not exist. There were vast plantations and belles named Scarlett, white-columned mansions, and "poor white trash." But the "Old North State" in the antebellum period was a land of yeomen farmers rather than gallant planters, of free Negroes as well as slaves, and of corn and livestock in addition to tobacco and cotton. Though there were some three hundred plantations in the state in 1860 of a thousand acres or larger, there were more than forty-six thousand farms of less than one hundred acres each. If the economic, political, and social influence of the larger planters outweighed their numerical proportion, in terms of life-style they represented an anomaly. In contrast to the multistory manor house of Greek Revival design, the dwelling on the average farm was a three-room log or frame structure conceived and constructed by the occupants themselves.

For a large number of Carolinians, however, plantation life did represent a norm. Approximately a third of the state's population was enslaved, and of this group over half were held by planters who owned twenty slaves or more. Although most bondsmen had little occasion to participate directly in the affairs of the "Big House," it was the slave community around which life on the plantation largely revolved.

The Planters

Somerset Place State Historic Site in Washington County offers a provocative glimpse of life among the planter elite in the antebellum South. Begun in the late eighteenth century, the plantation was largely the creation of Josiah Collins of Edenton, who had emigrated from England in 1773 and had made a fortune as a merchant during the American Revolution. Along with two partners whom he later forced to sell out, Collins formed the Lake Company to develop the desolate and, at the time, worthless swamplands bordering Lake Phelps. The company arranged for a direct shipment from Africa of eighty slaves, who were put to work digging a canal twenty feet wide from the lake to the Scuppernong River, a distance of six miles. Upon completion of the three-year project, a large estate was drained and cleared, grist- and sawmills were constructed along the canal, and the company began gradually divesting itself of the hundred thousand acres it had acquired in the area.

Though Collins and later his son, Josiah II, maintained their residence and mercantile business in Edenton, they retained a meticulous interest in Somerset and its continued development. Thus, when twenty-one-year-old Josiah Collins III assumed control of the

plantation in 1830, he inherited not only thousands of acres of arable land and almost three hundred slaves with whom to maintain it, but also a brilliantly designed system of waterways and water-powered labor-saving devices that made the agricultural operation one of the most technologically advanced in the South. Originally conceived as a drainage and irrigation system for rice culture, the network of secondary canals served as a versatile means of transport when in the early nineteenth century the Collinses shifted to the large-scale production of corn. Huge barges could be floated alongside the fields during planting and harvest to move bulk quantities of the crop to and from the storage barns and processing plant located on the main canal. Yet it was the ingenuity of the processing mechanism itself that

Somerset Place (ca. 1830), near Scuppernong, Washington County, was named for Josiah Collins's birthplace in England.

Stonewall Plantation, Rocky Mount (Falls Road, N.C. #43 and #48), Nash County, overlooking the Tar River, shows the opulence of the finest antebellum houses.

Robert Hunter, Jr., a young London merchant who was visiting Edenton in June 1785, wrote in his diary: "Mr. Allan [a partner of Collins] has a brig arrived today from the coast of Guinea. She has only been seven months on her passage out and home and has a hundred slaves aboard in the state of nature (women and men). They talk a most curious lingo, are extremely black, with elegant white teeth. They shipped corn to Guinea, which turned out to a great profit, and the Negroes at twenty-eight pounds sterling by that means did not stand them in near the money. They are all from twenty to twenty-five years of age. Mr. Allan has bought them to drain a lake on the other side of the sound (which was discovered about thirty years ago) by digging a canal seven miles long. He expects to finish it by Christmas if it ceases raining . . . in keeping 150 slaves daily at work. The expense, he says, will be 3,000 at least, but when the work is accomplished he will have cleared 100,000 acres of the finest woodland that almost was ever known (oak, sycamore, poplar, cypress, etc.)—which is an amazing object and a very great undertaking."

Port records show that instead of a hundred slaves the brig brought only eighty.

Slaves planting rice.

impressed visitors such as Edmund Ruffin, the noted agricultural editor and reformer, who explained the procedure in 1838 as follows:

> When it is desired to prepare a cargo of corn for the Charleston market, there is no need of commencing until notice has been received of the vessel having arrived in the river below. The shelling of the corn is then commenced, by a shelling machine of immense power, then fanned, next lifted up by elevating machinery, from the first to the fourth story of the house, there measured, and then emptied through a spout into a large flatboat lying in the canal, which, as soon as loaded in bulk, is conveyed along the canal to the vessel. Thus the risk of keeping a large quantity of shelled corn in bulk is avoided, and by the aid of water, all the operations necessary to load a vessel may be completed in a very short time.

Life at Somerset for young Collins and his family was quite profitable in an economic sense, yet the costs of their existence in the region must not be overlooked. Though the environment of Lake Phelps and the surrounding swamps proved to be as abundant as it was hauntingly beautiful, it could be a liability as well. Travel to and from the plantation was difficult, time-consuming, and sometimes dangerous. Overland transport by horse, cart, or carriage meant traversing roads that were often little more than muddy footpaths in addition to fording the numerous streams that dissected the low-lying area. Water travel required following the circuitous route down the main canal and along the slow-moving river before facing the contrary winds and shifting shoals of Albemarle Sound. Edenton, the nearest town of any consequence, was a full day's journey away—that is, if the weather held.

Frequent storms and even occasional droughts multiplied the problems at the plantation itself. Floods washed away dikes along the canals and the lake, high winds flattened the corn and uprooted trees, hail destroyed crops as they stood in the field, and lightning periodically ignited fires in the nearby swamps. On several occasions livestock were drowned and various outbuildings were inundated as a result of severe weather. A hurricane that struck in 1839 reportedly raised the lake level six feet in several hours and left water standing as high as the ridges in the cornfields.

Another common feature of life at Somerset Place was illness and death. Malaria, generally known at the time as "ague," was endemic. Since there was no effective cure, the sufferer could merely hope to minimize its recurring symptoms of chills and fever. The threat of smallpox and cholera epidemics repeatedly reached the lake region. And in 1839 what was termed "epidemic influenza" raged in the area, frequently causing its victims to rave for several days before the relief of recovery or death. "Flux" (dysentery), "consumption" (tuberculosis), rheumatism, and skin cancer were also common complaints. But often as dangerous as the diseases that threatened every member of the community were the accidents that occurred during day-to-day plantation activity. Snake bites, serious cuts, crushed or broken limbs—injuries of all types were a constant concern and, as the Collinses were well aware, could result in permanent disability or even worse. Edward and Hugh Collins, aged eight and ten, along with two black playmates drowned in 1843 in the murky water of the main canal. And several years later a third son, William, died in a riding accident on the carriageway leading to the house.

Only slightly less obvious than the physical hazards of their dismal environment was the social and psychological isolation that the Collinses felt at Somerset. Educated in the North, Josiah III thrived on the cosmopolitan atmosphere and cultural amusements available to the wealthy in such cities as Boston and New York. His wife, Mary Riggs Collins, was a native of New Jersey and maintained close ties of family and friendship in northern society. Thus the Collinses felt little affinity with the increasing number of small farmers who moved into the region and were occasionally hired to supplement the labor force at Somerset Place. Surprisingly, a similar coolness characterized the Collinses' relationship with the distinguished Pettigrew family, who owned the adjacent plantation of Bonarva. Ebenezer Pettigrew, who was almost fifty when Josiah III and his bride took up permanent residence at the lake, had devoted his entire life to the careful development of his property in the region. As intractable as he was conscientious, Pettigrew regarded his young neighbor as something of a dilettante planter; Collins for his part imperiously rejected Pettigrew's views on almost every topic from politics to religion. Though the two families maintained a polite cordiality, their relationship was marred by pettiness, jealousy, and outright competition.

Still it would seem difficult to be lonely in the midst of what actually constituted a sizable community of over three hundred people living and working on the plantation. Undoubtedly the Collinses did develop a close personal relationship with many of those individuals with whom they were in day-to-day contact. Yet the fact remains that the antebellum slaveholder was bound to a brutal system of perpetual exploitation that could only be maintained by the constant threat of violent force. Consequently the Collinses found themselves surrounded by a people whose labor they could not afford to be without, but whose very presence posed a potential danger to livelihood, lifestyle, and even life itself.

The Collinses responded to the environment confronting them at Somerset in ways that were typical of the planter class throughout the South. Shortly after their arrival in 1830, Josiah III and Mary began an extensive renovation and expansion of the plantation house

Josiah Collins III (1808–63). Portrait by William G. Brown, owned by Mrs. Frank Williams. Photograph by Charles Clark. N.C. State Archives.

Ebenezer Pettigrew (1783–1848). Photograph by Walton Haywood. N.C. State Archives.

Mrs. Pettigrew observed that "the education of the [Collins] son will cause him to pass many a wretched hour, it will be very unlike New York, the opera and amusements of various kinds which that great city affords." Lemmon, ed., *Pettigrew Papers*.

Dining room, Somerset Place. Together at mealtimes, the family spoke French with the help of a resident tutor.

that stands today on a magnificent site overlooking Lake Phelps. The rear wing and broad porches that now characterize the structure were added a decade later, creating a mansion almost triple the size of the original dwelling. The house was sumptuously decorated with the finest available furniture, imported carpets and fabrics, and costly works of art. An inventory compiled in 1839 listed some 60 chairs, numerous chests and cabinets, and 3 large dining tables. The accessories in the dining room alone included a 151-piece set of fine gold and white china, over 100 knives and forks, 10 carving sets, and 16 decanters.

The aura of stability, wealth, and power created by the mansion was complemented by the order imposed upon the surrounding natural landscape. The front of the house was parallel with the main canal and perpendicular to the shore of the lake. A row of stately oaks stood along the broad levee that bounded the canal and doubled as a carriageway leading to the entrance of the estate. A formal English garden was planted next to the house and adjacent to a group of several outbuildings, some of which were reoriented to create a more aesthetically pleasing setting for the expanded mansion. Across the canal in what had once been a tangled jungle of dense vegetation was an open lawn of several acres surrounded by large shade trees and an oval race course. Completing the patterned arrangement of the plantation complex was a uniform row of slave cabins that began some distance from the rear of the main house and extended in an uninterrupted line along the lake and down a secondary canal.

Yet for the Collins family not even the opulence of the mansion at Somerset could offset the social, cultural, and physical isolation of life on Lake Phelps. Consequently they thrived on the visits of relatives and friends, who often stayed for weeks and were always lavishly entertained. Even the Pettigrews remarked on the "energy" their neighbors displayed "in catering for the amusement of their numerous guests." Though they considered the Collinses' hospitality to be aimed as much at overwhelming as entertaining their visitors, the Pettigrew family was ordinarily represented at the formal receptions, elegant dinners, and lively quadrilles that the Collinses held in honor of their guests.

The Collinses were also extremely concerned with maintaining an atmosphere of cultural refinement. Not only did they own an excellent library, but they also organized a reading club that met during the winter months for several years. The periodic sessions, which typically consisted of reading aloud, along with interludes of music and singing, included any guests who happened to be in residence at Somerset as well as several of the younger members of the Pettigrew family. Their appreciation of music was such that the Collinses felt they needed two pianos in the humid climate of the region; thus one would always be available for use while the other was in Norfolk being tuned. Yet the most remarkable of the Collinses' cultural endeavors occurred in 1845 when Josiah III hired a French tutor with the intention of adopting French as "the language of the house."

Despite the Collinses' elaborate efforts to compensate for the dangers and deficiencies of their life at Somerset, the only effective way to ease their dilemma was to escape. The family spent several months of every year touring the fashionable summer resorts and springs in Virginia and the North: White Sulphur, Saratoga, and others. Rarely did they pass up additional opportunities to get away on business or pleasure, even during the most critical seasons in the agricultural cycle. In fact Ebenezer Pettigrew came to consider Josiah III's extended absences a dereliction of duty that would ultimately lead to the young planter's ruin. When in 1835 severe weather was causing considerable damage to the crops in the area, Pettigrew mused: "[Mrs. Collins] stays on the Lake scarcely any and Mr. C. not much more. These things must needs be. But, woe unto him. . . ."

Company made isolation bearable.

Flat Rock, in the mountains of Henderson County, became the favorite resort of South Carolina planters, while Nag's Head, in Dare County on the coast, was beginning to develop as a resort for North Carolina planters. Woodfields Inn, Flat Rock, originally called Farmer's Hotel, dates from this period.

Lebanon Plantation slave cabin,
Averasboro vicinity, Harnett County.

The Slaves

Though they too felt the anxieties and suffered the hazards of plantation life, enslaved Carolinians had no viable means of escape. For it was not just their masters who subjected Afro-American slaves to bondage, nor the various overseers, patrollers, and slave catchers who kept the system intact. The crucial factor sustaining slavery in the antebellum South was the acquiescence of the overwhelming majority of southern whites. In spite of the fact that some 70 percent of white families in North Carolina owned no slaves, most nonslaveholders condoned the subjugation of black Americans, whom they considered part of a subordinate race. Thus arrayed against the slave who attempted to question or alter his status was the full weight of a dominant white society, convinced of his inferiority and prepared to use force to keep him in his place. That American slaves transcended the physical punishment and psychological abuse that slavery entailed is a tribute to the resilience of the Afro-American community in the face of the repressive conditions it has so often confronted.

The material remains of slave life in North Carolina are all but gone. Yet on a gentle knoll in Durham County, surrounded by the fields and forests known as Horton Grove, several weatherworn structures stand as a reminder of the vital culture that Afro-American slaves developed in the state. Now part of the Stagville Preservation Center, Horton Grove in the mid-nineteenth century was a productive component of the vast estate owned by the powerful Bennehan and Cameron families. The four substantial but decaying dwellings, which can be visited at the site, housed a portion of the hundreds of slaves who worked the Bennehan-Cameron properties and formed a cohesive community with roots in the colonial period and descendants in the region to this day.

The Bennehan and Cameron families, who were linked by business partnership as well as marriage, were among the wealthiest in the state. Paul C. Cameron, on whom the management of their combined holdings devolved in the decades prior to the Civil War, was known for his conscientiousness as a planter and his willingness to adopt innovative agricultural techniques. But the primary source of any planter's success, whether a Cameron in the Carolina Piedmont or a Collins on the Coastal Plain, was the industry and labor provided by the plantation labor force. Ebenezer Pettigrew begrudgingly acknowledged this debt: "Negroes are a troublesome property, and unless well managed, an expensive one, but they are indispensable in this unhealthy and laborious country, for these long canals, that are all important in rendering our swamplands valuable, must be dug by them or not at all."

Working from dawn to dusk, six days a week, slave laborers throughout the South accomplished the arduous and irksome tasks

associated with the large-scale production of staple crops. What is often overlooked in this day of mechanized agriculture is the skill and effort required to cultivate successfully such crops as cotton, tobacco, rice, corn, and wheat. Not only were lowlands like those surrounding Lake Phelps drained, but thousands of acres had to be cleared of massive trees, dense underbrush, and exposed rock. The process according to one observer could take as much as thirty man/days per acre, and given the continued demand for the high yields that rich "new soil" afforded, clearing additional acreage was an annual necessity.

Correct plowing, planting, and cultivating were also essential for a bountiful harvest. Each crop required varying levels of care and agricultural techniques. Corn demanded from one to three replantings to ensure a good stand against the ravages of cutworms, deer, and severe weather. The sprouting crop had to be thinned and hoed at least twice and finally "hilled" by pulling loose dirt around each stalk to provide additional support. Tobacco was started in carefully prepared seedbeds, then transferred plant by plant into the fields. In addition to normal cultivation, each plant required "priming" by stripping away several leaves at its base, "topping" by pinching off the top of the stalk when a sufficient number of leaves had developed, and "suckering" by removing the extraneous shoots that grew at the base of the leaves. The procedure not only depended on the experi-

The community of slave cabins, the "Quarter," kept black culture alive.

Unusually large and well-built slave houses (ca. 1851) at Horton Grove, Stagville Plantation, Durham County.

15

Slave worming tobacco.

One of the few remaining cotton presses may be seen on Tarboro town common at Albemarle St., Edgecombe County.

ence and judgment of the slave work force but required numerous trips over the same fields throughout the growing season.

Harvest was the most difficult and taxing period in the agricultural cycle. The entire plantation community contributed to the concentrated effort, and work invariably continued for sixteen to twenty hours a day until the job was completed. Only those crops brought in at the peak of their development could command the highest prices. Bad weather was the primary concern, for not only did it slow the harvest, but it endangered the crop as well. A storm could flatten a field of wheat, and even if it could be reaped the wetness made threshing almost impossible. Grain allowed to lie cut on damp ground was likely to be ruined by sprouting.

Although planting more than one staple crop multiplied the labor and the problems associated with agricultural production, a versatile work force allowed the planter to spread his economic risk through diversification. The field hands on the Bennehan-Cameron properties in the 1850s were responsible for producing vast quantities of tobacco, corn, and wheat for the market in addition to growing cotton, oats, rye, and flax largely for plantation use. At the same time, Bennehan-Cameron slaves were charged with the care of several hundred swine, sheep, and beef cattle, as well as numerous horses, mules, and other livestock essential to the estate's operation.

From curing tobacco to butchering hogs, the processing of agricultural products was also handled almost entirely by skilled slave labor. Bondsmen ran the intricate processing plant at Somerset, just as a slave mechanic named Ben Sears managed the threshing machine owned by Paul Cameron. A slave miller known as Cyrus operated the Cameron's grist-mill in Person County, while Matthew, who was owned by the Bennehans, directed their mill in Orange.

Yet the competence and proficiency of the enslaved labor force went beyond the production of agricultural products. By providing the basic goods and services necessary for day-to-day operation, slave artisans made many larger plantations virtually self-sufficient. Slave blacksmiths designed and repaired tools and essential iron implements, while coopers constructed the various wooden containers, from buckets to hogsheads, required for storage and shipment. Carpenters and masons built and repaired plantation buildings with materials furnished by sawyers and brickmakers. Enslaved spinners, weavers, tailors, and seamstresses provided the community with clothing, and tanners, cobblers, and harnessmakers supplied shoes and other essential leather goods. A mulatto bondsman named Virgil Bennehan served as a doctor for his fellow slaves on the Bennehan-Cameron estate, while a Pettigrew servant known as Airy acted as a nurse and a midwife for black and white alike.

Many bondsmen even took part in plantation management. The employment of black foremen known as "drivers" was a common

practice throughout the South. Responsible for work gangs of from ten to thirty hands, the foremen directed agricultural operations in the field. Although placed in an ambiguous position between the labor force and upper-level management, the driver had the opportunity to intercede on behalf of his own people as well as the obligation to carry out the instructions of his overseer or owner. On several plantations a slave actually served as the overseer. A bondsman named Jim Ray managed one of the Bennehan-Cameron properties in Person County, while at Lake Phelps, William S. Pettigrew entrusted the operation of the plantations he had inherited from his father, Ebenezer, to two slave overseers, Moses at Belgrade and Henry at Magnolia.

The material quality of life for slaves in antebellum North Carolina was directly related to their owner's wealth, humanity, and economic self-interest. Theories as to what constituted adequate housing, clothing, and diet for slave labor were almost as numerous as planters themselves. The dwellings that remain today at Horton Grove represent the best in a broad spectrum that ranged from shabby hovels with dirt floors and leaky roofs to the sweltering attics

The great barn at Horton Grove (1860), Durham County, called by Paul Cameron, its builder, "the best stables ever built in Orange (at Stagville) 135 feet long covered with Cypress shingles at a cost of $6 per thousand."

Butchering hogs.

Slave carpenter "Uncle Haywood" Dixon. Tintype courtesy Bill Murphy. A favorite slave of the Dixon family of Sandy Loam Plantation, Greene County, he and his family are buried in the white family graveyard. True to African tradition, blacks commonly used "uncle," "aunt," "sister," and "brother" to express respect or endearment.

and musty basements of the "Big House." Paul Cameron's major concern in regard to slave housing was that it provide a disease-free environment for his work force, thereby reducing the expense of slave illness. The quarters at Horton Grove, which were constructed by slave craftsmen in the early 1850s, were the culmination of decades of gradual improvements aimed primarily at increasing labor efficiency.

Similar to housing projects of a more modern age, the four buildings at Horton Grove are of identical design and construction and stand in a single row behind an earlier house that likely served as an overseer's residence. The two-story frame structures are built on pilings, and their thick exterior walls are filled with brick nogging covered by board-and-batten siding. On each floor are two rooms divided by a passageway that contains a narrow flight of stairs. Each of the four chambers is approximately seventeen feet square and has two windows and one large fireplace.

Each of the rooms in the dwellings at Horton Grove housed an entire slave family. Furnishings were sparse and consisted primarily of those items that family members could make or obtain for themselves. A crude table served as the center of domestic activity, a discarded chair provided an honored seat for an elderly relative, and a woven mat or shuck mattress offered a convenient if uncomfortable place to rest. The whitewashed walls were functionally ornamented with hanging pans and baskets, strings of drying herbs or fruit, and maybe even a conjurer's mark or talisman meant to ward off unwelcome visitors as well as evil spirits. Ebenezer Pettigrew allowed his bondsmen to exchange products grown or crafted in their limited free time for household and personal goods in his plantation store. In addition to such essentials as cooking utensils, plates, and bowls, slave purchases included small pieces of furniture, mirrors, and colorful curtain material, all of which helped to transform a dreary room into a warm if Spartan home.

Food and clothing were generally allocated to enslaved Carolinians in family units. Josiah Collins III, who like Cameron was comparatively generous in providing for his slaves, directed that they be clothed as follows: "They are to have Two good Suits of Clothes—one for Summer, and one of good woolen cloth for Winter—two pair of good double-soled shoes and one pair of woolen Stockings, one good wool hat [and] a Blanket not less than six feet long. A woman having one child is to have a Blanket for such child; when a woman has more than one child a Blanket is to be supplied for every two children; where the number of children in any one family is an odd number, then a Blanket is to be supplied for such child also."

As in their dwellings, any embellishment or addition to the coarse uniform that bondsmen were issued was the result of their own enterprise. Again Pettigrew's account book indicated that de-

Henry Dixon and his wife, Mary Sugg Dixon, owners of Haywood Dixon. Tintype courtesy Bill Murphy.

mand for such items as buttons, handkerchiefs, stockings, shoes, and cloth such as calico and gingham was quite high. A slave named Will, for example, worked to buy some cotton stockings for his wife, while Pompey saved enough to purchase a shawl and a pair of shoes for his.

Whenever possible bondsmen attempted to supplement their meager food allotment as well. Corn and pork were the dietary staples for most of the slave population in North Carolina. Normally at the beginning of each week, every family was provided with several pounds of hog meat and a peck of cornmeal for each of its members. Periodically those planters who considered it essential to the maintenance of their slaves' strength substituted beef for pork and included a measure of molasses along with any available vegetables. Though such a regimen supplied sufficient calories to meet the demands of a strenuous workday, it was woefully lacking in the vitamins and protein necessary for proper development and good health. Most enslaved families augmented their ration in some way, whether by hunting, gathering, fishing, or theft. Many were allowed to cultivate their own gardens and maintain livestock in what little spare time they had. But despite their efforts bondsmen were rarely in adequate physical shape to resist common respiratory and intestinal ailments. And they were regularly afflicted with a variety of complaints, from skin irritations and visual impairment to rickets and pellagra, now associated with dietary deficiency.

"Aunt Sarah" Pleasants Taylor, another Dixon slave, was born "fore de stars fell" (1838 meteor shower). Photograph courtesy Bill Murphy.

Yet slavery in the antebellum South involved more than toil, disease, and death. It meant the sexual exploitation of black women, the brutal punishment of black men, and the arbitrary rending of black families as well. The resilience that enabled Afro-Americans to withstand the persecution that enslavement entailed stemmed from their development of a distinctive culture that served to mitigate the physical abuse and offset the psychological degradation. It was in the "Quarter," not the "Big House," that bondsmen found their social and moral frame of reference. Drawing on both African heritage and American experience, the slave community evolved its own system of values and ideals and created the vital cultural forms that fostered and sustained them. Religion, music, and folklore all helped promote solidarity, build self-esteem, and perpetuate hope. But the foundation of slave culture was the family.

The overwhelming majority of enslaved Carolinians chose to live in family units cemented by the monogamous relationship of husband and wife. Although slave marriages were not legally recognized anywhere in the South, most masters accepted the practice as a settling influence on their bondsmen as well as a means of expanding their work force through natural increase. The slave's family surrounded him with the love and support necessary to endure the oppression of plantation life and passed on the traditions and skills required to survive with his identity intact. It was the bondsman's wife who massaged his tired muscles with her own aching fingers after a long day's work, just as it was the assurance of a knowing grandparent that restored the courage of the frightened child whose mother was being whipped.

The significance that slaves attached to familial ties was evident in their names. Despite the fact that it was customary to adopt the surname of one's current owner, many bondsmen tenaciously clung to a former name, whether of African or American derivation, which identified them with their own lineage. Given names too indicated a desire to reinforce the sustaining bond of kinship. Approximately 40 percent of the children in the Bennehan-Cameron slave community bore the first name of a beloved aunt, uncle, or other member of their extended family.

The old man who spun allegorical tales in the quarter on warm summer nights was also an agent of Afro-American culture. The misadventures of a "Br'er Rabbit," who depended on guile and valor to outwit, if only temporarily, his powerful antagonists, brought more than smiles to a perceptive slave audience. Patterned after the folklore of their African past, the stories dealt creatively with the realities of their American present. Though intended to entertain, the imaginative tales provided a source of encouragement as well as a means of covertly expressing hostility. Often the strategies utilized by characters such as "Trickster John," who cleverly manipulated his adver-

Slaves were often permitted to cultivate their own gardens in their free time. N.C. State Archives.

George Moses Horton, a Chatham County slave, wrote poetry and sold his services to Chapel Hill students, who saw no irony in paying a black man to do their literary wooing for them. For himself he wrote:

"How long have I in bondage lain,
    And languished to be free!
Alas! and I still complain—
    Deprived of liberty."

saries by pretending to be ignorant and humble, could be directly applied to the bondsmen's own situation.

Music was another creative outlet that often had radical implications. An account of its significance for the original Collins slaves, who had been subjected to the horrors of the "Middle Passage" in order to dig the initial canal in the pestilent swamps surrounding Lake Phelps, was recorded by a nineteenth-century historian: "At night they would begin to sing their native songs, and in a short while would become so wrought up that, utterly oblivious to the danger involved, they would grasp their bundles of personal effects, swing them on their shoulders, and setting their faces toward Africa, would march down into the water of the Lake singing as they marched till recalled to their senses only by the drowning of some of the party. The owners lost a number of them in this way, and finally had to stop the evening singing."

Although the countless songs, both secular and religious, composed by American bondsmen were not generally intended to spark such a drastic reaction, the ideas they evoked were often as revolutionary in their effect. Music offered a psychological if not a physical release through which slaves could vent their emotion and verbalize their aggression. Thus it was employed to satirize subtly an evil master or condemn blatantly the inequity of plantation life.

Some slaves were literate, like this one reading to his daughter.

21

Spirituals as well were regularly used to communicate such subversive concepts as equality and freedom. In the classic "Go Down, Moses," which recounts in some twenty verses the Biblical story of the Israelites' deliverance from Egypt, there was little doubt as to whose "people" Afro-American slaves were actually referring:

When Israel was in Egypt's land,
O let my people go!
Oppressed so hard they could not stand,
O let my people go!
CHORUS—O go down Moses
Away down to Egypt's land,
And tell King Pharaoh
To let my people go!

Religion in itself was central to slave culture. Some plantation owners, such as the Collinses and Camerons, built chapels for their bondsmen and brought in white missionaries to preach. The slaveholders' concern for the spiritual well-being of their black "family," however, tended to manifest itself in an emphasis on the authoritarian and paternalistic aspects of Christianity. Lunsford Lane, a North Carolinian who was fortunate enough to purchase his freedom in the 1830s described the sermons he had heard as a slave: "So great was the similarity of the texts that they were always fresh in my memory: 'Servants, be obedient to your masters'. . . . 'He that knoweth his master's will and doeth it not, shall be beaten with many stripes;' and some others of this class. Similar passages, with but few exceptions, formed the basis of most of these public instructions. The first commandment was to obey our masters, and the second like unto it: labor as faithfully when they or the overseers were not watching, as when they were."

Infused by a vibrant spiritual heritage and vitalized by more radical Christian tenets, such as the brotherhood of man, Afro-American slaves developed their own brand of religion. In the intimacy of secret "hushharbors" deep in the woods, with wet blankets hung from branches to muffle the sound, bondsmen sang and shouted to the glory of an all-powerful though benevolent God who would succor them in slavery and deliver them to freedom, in this world as well as the next.

Their distinctive culture not only instilled in black Carolinians the will to endure slavery but the resolution to resist. The most powerful weapon the slave community possessed was its potential to disrupt agricultural production. The economic success of any plantation was dependent on its smooth and efficient operation. Yet there were any number of actions that bondsmen could take, either individually or collectively, to sabotage its function. It was easy "inadvertently" to break a hoe on an unnoticed rock, "unknowingly" to chop down the young plants along with the weeds, or "accidentally" to drop a hammer into the mechanism of a mechanical thresher. An individual slave could feign illness or pretend to misunderstand the simplest instructions, while the community, as a whole or in part, could hold up production with a work slowdown.

Obviously laborers who subverted plantation operations risked punishment that might range from whipping, to the assignment of more onerous tasks, to a reduction in rations. Ebenezer Pettigrew charged the cost of breakage and other damage done by his slaves to their accounts in his plantation store. Bondsmen did have the advantage of knowing that, except in the most extreme cases, their owners could not afford to inflict permanent physical harm. Besides, not even the most conscientious of masters or overseers could possibly keep tabs on their every action.

Theft too was rampant. Slaves stole from the plantation storehouses on their own and other plantations to supply personal needs as well as to participate in the clandestine "black market" that flourished in most parts of the South. For example, Pettigrew's father warned him: "In regard to your wheat, I am afraid it is too much exposed to the thievishness of the negroes. It is a very ready article of trade, & Fortune [a slave foreman at Bonarva] has his mercantile correspondents, who are ready at all times to receive him kindly."

Yet the most valuable property that a bondsman could steal was himself. For a successful escape not only resulted in the master's loss of a considerable capital investment, it also renewed the hope of freedom in the entire slave community. The odds against a runaway slave in the antebellum South were overwhelming, but undoubtedly the most important deterrent was the fact that escape meant leaving behind friends, relatives, and often even one's spouse and children. Numerous runaways never attempted to leave the region in which their families were located, while others chose to join the large "maroon" communities that inhabited desolate areas such as the Dismal Swamp. A Pettigrew bondsman named Dave hid for over two years in remote parts of Jones and Craven counties. Some slaves did reach the relative security of the northern states, where they were free from bondage but rarely from racial prejudice. Mary Walker, who was owned by Paul Cameron's sister, escaped to Philadelphia and was soon followed by her eldest son, Frank. Her mother and two children remained enslaved in North Carolina and some time later she prevailed on a friend to write a poignant inquiry about their purchase:

> I have come to know one Mary Walker formerly in your family, and I have seen how sick at heart she is about her mother [Siller] and expecially her two children [Agnes and Briant]. . . . Her motherheart yearns unspeakably after them and her eyes

100 Dollars Reward.

RAN away in July 1847, a negro man by the name of BUCK. He is yellow complexion, about five feet six inches high, rather bow-legged, very quick in his movements, and when spoken to very slow to answer. He was in the possession of Robert F. Morris, at Hillsborough, when he went away, and is very likely still in that neighborhood; yet he was raised in Granville county, by Mrs. Blacknall, in the neighborhood of Winton, and may be in that neighborhood now. The above reward will be given for his apprehension, and delivery to me; or confinement in any jail so that I can get him.

WM. J. HAMLETT.
Mount Tirza, Person, N. C., Jan. 29.   —66

Hillsborough Recorder, 21 February 1849. A runaway slave faced certain punishment when caught.

fail with looking towards the South, over the dreary interval which separates them from her. She has saved a considerable sum of money to buy them, can command more from friends, and will sacrifice anything to see them once again and have their young lives renew the freshness of her own weary spirit.

Apparently the Camerons were ummoved, for Agnes and Briant continued in bondage until the Civil War.

Slaveholders in North Carolina often punished chronic runaways and troublemakers by sale, not into the freedom of the North but into the brutality of the expanding "Cotton Kingdom" in the lower South. Aside from further attempts at escape, the bondsman's options for countering such action were few. Suicide was not uncommon nor physical retaliation, though both were likely to lead to the same end. A slave could threaten the life of his master if he was willing to die himself. Fire and poison were also available to avenging bondsmen, thus precluding the necessity of an overt assault. Cameron's grandfather was the target of a poisoning attempt, and his in-laws' house was set on fire by a house servant while his wife was there for a visit. But the greatest fear of planters throughout the South was large-scale slave revolt. Though never successful in an absolute sense, "conspiracies" and "uprisings" occurred just often enough to incite terror in the white population of the state and to inspire courage in the black.

Nevertheless it was life, not death, toward which the resistance of slaves was generally directed. Their willingness to resist mitigated the suffering to which they were subjected. Enslaved Carolinians utilized the threat of sabotage and violence not only to secure the social space necessary for their culture to flourish but also to force practical improvements in their living and working conditions. The Pettigrew slaves, for example, went on a rampage in 1836 when overseer Doctrine Davenport, in their master's absence, altered some of the more lenient plantation policies that Pettigrew had worked out with his labor force. Thefts multiplied, runaways increased, and even the slave foremen refused to obey direct orders. By the end of the year, Davenport reported: "The negrose has bothered me near to death . . . after keeping celebrating Christmas a week before I could get them to work I had to give them one thousand lashes." Even though Pettigrew upon his return quickly restored normal plantation routine, his slaves made certain that he never forgot the potential danger represented by their presence. In fact only weeks before he died, perhaps sensing the hollowness of his control, Pettigrew wrote: "I of late never go from here without being made sick . . . My negroes have within the last twelve months given me more trouble than in all the time I have been here before, & I see no end to it but with my life."

24

Farm Life

The majority of nineteenth-century North Carolinians knew neither the ostentatious gentility of the white-columned veranda nor the vivid counterculture of the "Quarters" stoop. The population of the state was comprised largely of ordinary farmers, rather than planters and slaves. Whether white yeoman or free black, landowner or agricultural laborer, most Tar Heels lived on small farms, over two-thirds of which in 1860 were composed of a hundred acres or less. Despite the pervading influence of the plantation, rural society was built around this broad middle class.

Although awareness of social gradations permeated the antebellum South, the economic hierarchy, at least for white Carolinians, was only loosely fixed. Examples of "rags to riches" success were rare, but it was not uncommon for a family, over several generations,

As the stage of a national event, the modest Bennett farmhouse, Durham County, looked like this to the *Harper's* illustrator.

to improve its standard of living and thereby its social status. If prosperity often seemed less a function of skill and energy than of opportunity, inclination, and luck, the possibility of achievement stimulated personal aspirations and industry. A day laborer could strive toward renting a plot of land to work for himself, while a tenant farmer and his wife might dream of purchasing a small farm of their own.

James and Nancy Bennett were one such couple whose determination and effort were rewarded. In their early forties, after years of toil, the Bennetts succeeded in purchasing a modest farm in what is now Durham County with some four hundred dollars of borrowed capital. Though in a real sense a monument to the perseverance and good fortune of this enterprising rural family, the Bennett Place State Historic Site stands today as a memorial to a momentous event over which the Bennetts ironically had no control. Because of its convenient location on the old road between Raleigh and Hillsborough, which linked the final position of the Confederate army under Joseph

E. Johnston to that of the Union army led by William T. Sherman at the close of the Civil War, the farm was chosen as the site at which to negotiate terms for surrender.

The reconstructed Bennett house and outbuildings provide more than a glimpse of the surroundings in which these two war-weary generals met in the days following Appomattox. For the life-style of the Bennetts, and of the many Carolinians who were so like them, is reflected in the simple but sturdy structures. It was Nancy Bennett who spent her mornings in the log kitchen contemplating next spring's garden or the afternoon's chores while she prepared her family's midday meal. James Bennett spent his evenings in the main room of the paneled frame (originally log) dwelling looking over the latest issue of the *Hillsborough Recorder* or smiling with his wife as they listened to one of their children recite a favorite Bible verse.

Though rural life in nineteenth-century North Carolina might well have been less hurried and complicated than that of today, it could also be quite rough. Nancy Bennett had already lost one husband when she married James in 1831. As the young farmer and his wife attempted to build a new life together, the state was engulfed in

a serious agricultural depression. One of nearly 40 percent of non-slaveholding farm families in the South who did not own the land they tilled, the Bennetts were particularly hard hit by the drop in agricultural prices. Forced to produce cash crops such as cotton or tobacco in order to pay their rent, tenant farmers were dependent on an unpredictable market over which they had absolutely no control. In a good year with heavy demand and a bumper crop, they might make a profit, but when the market was depressed it was almost impossible to avoid a loss. Consequently during the 1830s Bennett lost some twenty suits for debts totaling almost three hundred dollars, and on at least two occasions the court ordered his personal property seized in order to settle judgments against him.

In the following decade, as a result of their persistent efforts and a more favorable economic climate, the Bennetts fared somewhat better. The court appearances for debts ceased, and, though they still did not break even in every year, the family accounts for the entire period showed a profit of $30.74. More importantly, in 1846 the Bennetts purchased their farm. Though landownership entailed the burden of a considerable long-term debt, in terms of security and independence, it transformed their lives.

Unlike the larger planters and even most tenants, antebellum yeomen were typically more concerned with self-sufficiency than surplus profits. If a farm family could subsist on the goods produced on its own land by its own labor, the only costs incurred were taxes and mortgage payments. Thus most rural landowners concentrated both their acreage and energy on the production of the food crops necessary to feed themselves and their livestock and allotted only a portion of their arable land to products intended primarily for the market. After buying their farm, the Bennetts made the logical choice of growing foodstuffs such as corn or wheat as a cash crop and were thereby able to pay their debts with the same commodities that provided their nourishment.

Corn, because of its hardiness and versatility, was the most important crop on the Bennett farm. Inasmuch as it could be consumed on the cob, creamed, or roasted, as bread, hoecakes, grits, hominy, mush, or succotash, and indirectly as whiskey or pork, the grain served as the basis of the family's diet. Stalks and shucks also provided fodder for the livestock. Although maize could be planted in Carolina as early as March so as to avoid the annual summer drought, the Bennetts normally sowed their crop in April or May for an early fall harvest. Despite the general shift to row planting in the mid-nineteenth century, they persisted in planting their corn "Indian style" in hills. Thus, though Bennett prepared his fields with a horse-drawn plow, most of the cultivating was done by hand, using heavy grub hoes to form the soil into mounds. This back-breaking labor, however, usually paid off. For example, in 1847, in addition to supplying their needs for home consumption, the Bennetts sold eight bushels of corn for $3.67½, one-third bushel of cornmeal for $.20, 198½ pounds of fodder for $1.51¼, and $.05 worth of shucks.

Corn was only one of a number of agricultural products that the Bennetts produced. For diversification not only added a degree of variety to their diet; it helped protect them from the instability of the market. The Bennetts regularly grew oats and wheat, sweet and Irish potatoes, peas, and even watermelons for both home use and sale. And occasionally their garden yielded sufficient cucumbers, onions, squash, and turnips to be marketed along with the fruit of the apple and cherry trees that grew in the yard.

Livestock was also an integral part of the family's livelihood. As on many other southern farms, hogs provided the Bennetts with a primary source of both protein and profit. Because swine were generally branded and turned loose in the woods to forage on their own for two or three years, they were easy and inexpensive to raise. If penned and fattened before slaughter, they generally brought a reasonable market price. The Bennetts owned as many as seventeen hogs at one time, and during the decade of the 1840s their sales of pork, bacon, and lard totaled $77.45, which represented approximately 10 percent of their income.

A southern staple.

Other domestic animals served the Bennetts in a variety of ways. The chickens that scratched for food in the barnyard were sold periodically at a dime a head and thus offered a source of supplemental earnings as well as of eggs and meat. On the other hand, the products furnished by their small herd of cattle—milk, butter, cheese, and beef—were almost entirely consumed by the family itself. At least one horse provided the power necessary to plow the fields and transport surplus crops to market. Even family pets gave more to their masters than loyalty and love. A nimble cat was as essential to keeping the smokehouse and kitchen free of rodents as an alert dog was to a successful hunt.

Although the Bennetts largely succeeded in producing their own food supply, they had to clothe themselves as well. Before buying their farm they had grown cotton and even experimented with raising some sheep. Yet because they chose to concentrate their principal agricultural endeavors on foodstuffs, it was necessary to develop an alternative means of offsetting the expense of clothing. Though both ready-made garments and shoes were available at most country stores, the Bennetts began purchasing their own tailoring supplies and shoe leather as early as 1833. Working intensively during the winter months, when the demands of their farming operation were least, the family was not only able to dress itself but to manufacture additional coats, vests, pants, and shoes for sale. Though their clothing business seldom showed a profit, in terms of covering the costs of their own apparel the Bennetts did very well.

In a similar attempt to turn expense into income, James Bennett in 1845, after years of renting wagons from various neighbors for 25 cents a day, resolved to build one of his own. Though the vehicle cost almost $43 in parts and labor and took some six months to complete, it soon began to generate a substantial return. In addition to saving several dollars a year in rental fees, by the end of the decade the practical farmer had earned over $19 with his wagon through lending and hauling, including $1.95 for transporting 775 pounds of meal to Raleigh and $5.50 for conveying students and their luggage to and from the academies in Hillsborough.

Carrying passengers and freight was only one of many ways by which the Bennetts attempted to supplement their income. Taking advantage of their strategic location, they regularly sold horse feed and tobacco plugs to travelers and occasionally took in paying guests for a meal or even a night's lodging. A Mr. Cox, for example, paid forty cents for breakfast in January 1848, while the next month a pair of visitors were charged a dollar each for lodging and two meals. At times the family marketed liquor by the quart as well. After making almost a dollar profit on a five-dollar keg of brandy during 1847, the Bennetts repeated the venture using whiskey the following year.

Despite their best efforts, both agricultural and entrepreneurial,

nineteenth-century farmers were rarely able to attain total self-sufficiency or to neutralize all costs. The Bennetts and their fellow yeomen were becoming increasingly active participants in the expanding market economy of the state as consumers as well as producers. They were dependent on the nearby country store for staple goods such as salt, sugar, and coffee, just as they required the services of the local miller to grind their corn and the neighboring blacksmiths to repair their tools. And often during peak periods in the agricultural cycle the Bennetts had to employ day laborers to assist them on the farm itself.

Frequently the Bennetts were tempted by the broad spectrum of nonessential and even luxury items available to them as well. Their accounts included a wide variety of purchases, from exotic foodstuffs like coconut and lemonade to such popular products as shaving soap and Dr. Brandreth's Pills. The family seemed particularly partial to seafood as a means of diversifying their diet and often feasted on saltwater delicacies like oysters, herring, and shad. Books too were a special interest. Besides an annual almanac and several spelling and arithmetic texts for the children, their acquisitions included such works as *The Young Brides*, *The Lady at Home*, and a two-volume *Bible History*. On occasion the Bennetts were even known to splurge on a very special gift, like the bottle of cologne that James found for Nancy the year after their marriage or the parasol that the couple bought to surprise their fifteen-year-old daughter, Eliza.

As a result, in spite of their high degree of self-sufficiency and the diversity of their sources of income, the Bennetts were seldom totally out of debt. Although from the 1840s on they were generally able to repay what they owed with goods, services, or cash, their annual accounts for four of the ten years in the decade showed a loss. Still the Bennetts seemed satisfied with their lot.

They might well have fared better economically had they attempted to maximize their profits by concentrating entirely on the production of marketable staples, but such a course of action involved inherent risks. As landowners the Bennetts were not forced to place themselves at the mercy of the market merely to pay their rent. And unlike larger planters they simply did not have the capital to invest in more fertile land, technologically advanced implements and machinery, or improved agricultural techniques that could increase efficiency and thereby lower production costs. The substantial debt incurred by the purchase of a deeper plow or the stronger mule necessary to pull it would have jeopardized their hold on the farm itself. Thus the Bennetts, and thousands of Carolina yeomen like them, made do with what they had—employing the methods of their parents before them, basking in the warmth and love of their family and friends, and reveling in the independence and security afforded by working their own land.

Hillsborough Recorder, 21 February 1849.

In one of his carefully kept account books, James Bennitt wrote: "James Bennitt his Pocket Book Bought at Hillsborough July the 30th 1823" and later added:

> "Don't steel this Book
> for fear of shame
> for just above
> stands the owners name
> this the 18th day of March 1827."

Community Life

Conservative and self-sufficient as they may have been, nineteenth-century farm families like the Bennetts did not live their lives in isolation. Few weeks passed without the distraction of a trip to the local store, the stimulation of an enthusiastic religious gathering, or the conviviality of a neighborhood quilting bee. A strong sense of community pervaded rural life, buttressed by a tradition of social responsibility and communal interdependence. The expanding market economy and increasing political democracy of the Jacksonian era also encouraged active involvement in community affairs.

Commercial centers such as the country store and nearby grist-mill offered antebellum farmers more than essential goods and services. They provided a nucleus for community life. There rural Carolinians, whether planter or tenant, free black or white, converged to purchase supplies, grind their corn, or simply visit with neighbors and friends. The men seldom passed up the opportunity to discuss the prospects for their crops or exchange the latest political gossip, while their wives compared prices of newly available merchandise or laid plans for a forthcoming social event. If not playing near the millpond, the children could be found marveling at the whir of the mill machinery or gazing at the mouth-watering confectionery prominently displayed on the storekeeper's shelf.

The social and economic attraction of mills and stores made them the center of rural civic and political activity as well. While there one could pick up mail or read the numerous broadsides announcing estate sales, runaway slaves, camp meetings, horse races, or other matters of community interest. At the larger commercial centers, the county sheriff came at appointed times to collect taxes and the local militia met at least twice a year to train all morning and carouse all afternoon. Holidays and election days were celebrated there as well, with many a politician plying his constituents with powerful oratory and potent drink.

The backcountry merchants who operated the stores and the rural industrialists who owned the mills were often one and the same. Such was the case at West Point on the Eno River in Durham County, where Herbert Sims and later his stepson John McCown controlled a multifaceted complex that in the mid-nineteenth century included a general store, grist- and sawmills, a blacksmith shop, a cotton gin, a distillery, and a post office. The West Point gristmill, which once served a thriving community of some three hundred farm families, has been reconstructed on its original foundation and stands today in a Durham city park along with McCown's house and a working blacksmith shop.

Carolina yeomen, who worked so hard to earn their livelihood, were not only cautious about how they spent their money, but where.

West Point Mill, Durham, Durham County.

32

John Cabe McCown's house, Durham County, now part of West Point Mill Park restoration.

Consequently the business of supplying their commercial needs was quite competitive, and the more services an entrepreneur could offer the greater his chances of success. As with modern shopping centers, a convenient location was even more important than the range of products and services offered. It generally took hours, not minutes, to travel the miles to the nearest store or mill, even in the densely settled Piedmont. Thus, trading in a readily accessible location could save a farmer as much as half a day. Sims's West Point complex, for example, was built next to the north-south thoroughfare that crossed the Eno at Shoemaker's Ford and therefore had a substantial advantage over competitors that could be approached from only one side of the river.

The fact that its various owners had the political power necessary to ensure West Point adequate access and governmental patronage was also a major factor in the mill's successful operation for over a century and a half. Only a few years after it opened, the county government ordered a new road built to link the mill with Hillsborough. Sims, who was a colonel in the militia and a representative in the General Assembly as well as a large landowner, saw to it that a post office was established at the site. And its future seemed assured in 1851 when McCown and the community were able to exert sufficient pressure on the county court to authorize a bridge over the river at West Point.

With prices high and money scarce, it was necessary for storekeepers to offer antebellum farmers more than a good location in order to move their merchandise. The bulk of their goods, from farm implements to foodstuffs, had to be sold on credit or not at all. Accounts were secured by forthcoming crops and were normally settled once a year in the winter, when both harvesting and marketing were largely complete. It was not unusual for two-thirds or more of the proceeds from a farmer's marketable crops to go to the merchant. Many families, particularly those who were farm tenants, often had little or nothing left. Because they could pay their rent and other overdue accounts only by farming yet another year, they were forced deeper and deeper into debt.

The risk of extending liberal credit and the cost of overland transport occasioned markups in rural stores as high as 100 percent. Since buying on credit was the norm, no interest charges were added to the purchase price except on overdue accounts. Customers received a discount if they actually paid for their purchases at the time of the sale. Despite the merchant's substantial costs and considerable risks, returns were large, normally averaging around 70 percent. An item that sold for one dollar had likely been purchased for fifty cents. Because only about fifteen cents from the proceeds covered the storekeeper's operating costs, he was left with a profit of thirty-five cents. The overhead invested in stocking a store, however, could be quite high and the volume of sales was often very low. Thus, while numerous Tar Heels, like Paul Cameron's grandfather, Richard Bennehan, found storekeeping to be the way to wealth, not every owner became rich.

The amount of currency in circulation during the antebellum period was insufficient to function as the sole means of exchange. Consequently rural storekeepers were forced to accept agricultural products as payment for their merchandise. Typically the merchant turned the situation to his advantage. Because most Carolina yeomen lacked the time and money to travel to large markets, such as Fayetteville or Petersburg, they were dependent on the nearby store as the principal outlet for their cash crops. By concentrating the output of a large number of small producers and carefully selecting the market in which to trade, country storekeepers were generally able to obtain more for agricultural staples than they had allowed their customers and thus realize an additional profit.

Richard Mendenhall's store (1824), Jamestown, Guilford County. Kemp Battle related: "Near Greensborough we met an old acquaintance of my father, a refined and educated Quaker named Richard Mendenhall. On parting he said courteously, 'Come and see me, Kemp, and I will entertain thee for thy father's sake until I know thee and can entertain thee for thy own.'"

Few antebellum stores remain. Warren's store (ca. 1850), Prospect Hill, Caswell County, was a typical general store of the day, providing as well a post office and the clerks' lodgings.

Although attracted by the convenience of a local market and the availability of easy credit, it was primarily the merchandise that brought Carolinians to the country store. Whether a crude cabin along a mountain road or a two-story brick edifice in the more prosperous east, stores lured farm families by their curious blend of sights and smells, both familiar and unknown, and the pleasing array of a multitude of items from the essential to the extravagant. A broad range of foodstuffs tempted the palate: bags of fresh flour, barrels of salted meat, strings of dried fruit, tubs of homemade preserves, and jars of imported spices. Dry goods included bone buttons and metal needles, adjustable suspenders and felt hats, as well as bolts of material both gaily colored and drab. Washtubs, churns, oil lamps and all the latest appliances were available for the overworked housewife, along with an entire line of farm implements, from wooden pitchforks to iron plows, for the farmer himself. Harness, rope, paint, nails, powder, and shot could be found there too, as well as dictionaries, wedding rings, and often perfume. Some stores even carried spectacles to improve weak vision in addition to castor oil and epsom salts for ailing stomachs and one or more patent medicines guaranteed to cure everything from common colds to "Female Complaints."

Generally customers were more interested in having access to a wide variety of articles rather than a broad choice of quality and price, and storekeepers did their best to oblige. The merchandise carried reflected not only the rural character of the community served, but also its desire to sample what the outside world had to offer. A typical inventory might include Belgian lace, West Indian rum, Italian macaroni, or English novels along with butter, bacon, homespun, and whiskey that were locally produced. Because brand-names were few, yeomen were dependent on the character and competence of the merchant, as well as their own good judgment, to ensure the quality of their purchases.

In its dual capacity as a local market and community center, the country store was open from early in the morning till late at night. The storekeeper and his family often lived on the premises, so that regardless of the hour someone could always be found stocking the shelves, working on the books, sweeping the yard, or feeding the chickens in the nearby coop. And likely as not a customer or two would be there as well, trying on a starched collar, sampling a piece of cheese, or sharing a story over a pint of ale.

Gristmills also provided an essential economic service for the rural community. Not only was milling necessary to transform corn into meal and wheat into flour for human consumption, but also to reduce the cost of transporting these bulky agricultural commodities to market. The yield of an entire acre of corn could be reduced to around five barrels of meal, while a barrel of flour contained approximately five bushels of threshed wheat. In addition to decreasing the problems of transport, processed farm products generally brought a higher market price. It often paid southern planters or merchants who handled large quantities of staple crops to construct a gristmill, a cotton gin, or even a tobacco factory for their own use and that of the neighboring community.

Sims's mill at West Point incorporated numerous technological improvements that had been developed over centuries of milling. Built on a rock foundation, the three-story frame structure housed two runs of millstones, each of which could grind either corn or wheat. The power generated by the overshot waterwheel was transferred by a carefully devised series of pulleys and leather belts to the heavy cylindrical stones, which could be adjusted to control the texture of the product. The unground kernels and the ground flour as well moved between floors of the building through the entire process of grinding, sifting, and bagging along an ingenious system of gravity-dependent chutes and belt conveyors, also powered by the waterwheel. The intricate operation is still a pleasure to behold.

Laurel Mill on Sandy Creek, near Louisburg, Franklin County. Photograph by Randall Page. N.C. State Archives.

By the antebellum period, most mills were run by skilled artisans rather than the owners themselves. The job was both difficult and dangerous. It not only entailed a thorough knowledge of the mill's mechanics and the constant lifting of heavy bags of meal and flour, but it also required working constantly in a noisy, dust-filled environment and in close proximity to the heavy mill machinery, much of which was unprotected. Many millers were maimed or killed while attempting to free a frozen gear or to replace a worn mill stone, each of which weighed approximately a ton. Respiratory disease was simply accepted as an occupational hazard. Despite all the hazards, the miller's pay was relatively low, from $150 to $200 per year, and because many prosperous owners, like the Bennehans and the Camerons, depended on slaves to operate their mills, their labor costs were even less.

Rather than charging a fee for the service to local farmers who brought their wheat and corn to be ground, the miller assessed a toll of from one-twelfth to one-eighth of the resultant meal or flour. Like the rural store, returns in the milling business were high. When operating at full capacity, an efficient mill like West Point could grind up to six bushels of both corn and wheat in an hour. That translated into an income of approximately sixty dollars in a ten-hour working day and, after subtracting costs, could result in a profit of as much as two thousand dollars per year.

But there were also risks involved in operating a mill. The investment required was quite large. The West Point mill in 1860, for example, was valued at $6,500. In addition to the problem of fluctuating demand because of heavy local competition or poor crop yield, there was the constant threat of breakdowns or floods. A freshet could wash out the milldam or the waterwheel, and severe flooding could sweep away the building itself. As a result, the services of good millwrights were always at a premium. For, while the dam might be at least temporarily patched or a drive belt repaired within a few days, rebuilding an entire mill could take months.

Rural communities attracted numerous skilled artisans in addition to millers and millwrights. The services of a blacksmith, who had both the faculties and the facilities to repair farm tools and produce household implements more efficiently than the average yeoman, were becoming increasingly important to the successful operation of a nineteenth-century farm. James Bennett depended on nearby smiths not only to construct the more intricate parts of his wagon but to sharpen a grub hoe, mend a lock, or shoe a horse. Sawyers, threshers, ginners, and distillers, too, came to operate the expanding enterprises of rural entrepreneurs, as did storekeepers and clerks to run the country stores and teamsters and wagoners to transport agricultural products and commercial goods to and from distant markets.

Dr. Francis J. Kron's house and office, Morrow Mountain State Park, Stanly County. Kron was skilled in medicine and horticulture.

Interior of a blacksmith shop. N.C. State Archives.

An authentic blacksmith shop has been moved to the Greensboro Historical Museum, Guilford County.

Ministers and teachers were an integral part of rural society as well, for on an even more fundamental level than the local commercial center, churches and schools provided a focus for community life. Beyond the family, religious and educational institutions were most responsible for shaping antebellum Carolinians' consciousness and culture. The congregation and the classroom often encompassed the entire sphere of one's day-to-day acquaintances, and it was within this context that young and old alike were exposed to many of the ideas and much of the information on which their world view depended. Here too, while learning and laughing together on wintry mornings in a rustic schoolroom or worshiping and talking with one another in a shady churchyard in the sweltering summer heat, Tar Heels were likely to develop their most viable and intimate personal relationships.

Debate over the establishment of a system of public education in North Carolina raged throughout the antebellum period. The issue involved more than determining whether the family, the church, or the state should assume the primary responsibility for educating society's youth. It was inevitably linked to larger questions concerning the necessity of formal education and the proper role of government itself. Finally, the legislature in 1839 passed a bill calling for the development of a statewide school system supported by county taxes and appropriations from the "Literary Fund," which had been created for that purpose over a decade earlier. But, because of public apathy and inadequate direction, public education was not firmly established in North Carolina until the 1850s, and even then not in every county and only for whites.

Consequently the majority of rural schools in the state through

Ebenezer Academy, Bethany, near Statesville, Iredell County, dates from 1823. Photograph by Randall Page. N.C. State Archives. Besides the local children, pupils came from great distances. Board could be found for them "in respectable families at one dollar per week. Tuition proportionately low." Coon, *North Carolina Schools*.

the mid-nineteenth century were funded by private subscription and were the result of local initiative rather than statewide mandate. At times a number of concerned parents joined together to secure an instructor for their children, yet just as often subscription, or "old-field schools," were established through the efforts of the teachers themselves. For example, Mary Gash circulated the following proposal in the western North Carolina community of Burn's Creek:

> Mary A. Gash proposes to teach a school at Burn's Creek schoolhouse for the term of 3 months or 12 weeks commencing May 1857.
> Spelling Reading Writing and Arithmetic $2.40
> Geography English Grammar Philosophy & Composition . 3.60
> Astronomy Chemistry and Rhetoric 4.20
> She obligates herself to preserve good order so far as is within her power, and those who are not willing to be governed by the rules of the school may expect to be expelled.
> Twenty scholars are desired though she will commence with sixteen.
> The subscribers are expected to pay their tuition at the close of the school.

Though most rural communities supported a subscription school at one time or another, their tenuous existence depended on continued demand as well as the availability of a satisfactory teacher.

Capable and qualified instructors were rare. With the exception of a few well-educated ministers who supplemented their income by teaching and various university graduates who began their careers in the rural classroom, most primary school teachers were only marginally proficient in the three R's themselves. Pay was extremely low and in subscription schools often difficult to collect. More importantly, since the annual term was normally limited to only three or four months during the winter lull in the agricultural cycle, it was impossible to subsist solely by teaching. As a result, Calvin H. Wiley, state superintendent of public instruction, in 1853 offered the county school boards the following pragmatic advice: "I would suggest to you to encourage good teachers to locate permanently in the neighborhoods, as they can thus be more useful in creating and fostering a spirit of education, can have their salaries, in time increased by private subscriptions, and can also, in other respects make their vocation more profitable by cultivating farms or carrying on, or having carried on, other industrial or commercial occupations. Encourage as much as possible the very poor, and especially poor females to become teachers."

Recruitment and retention of competent teachers was not only inhibited by low salaries but by the heavy demands of the job itself. The school day extended from early morning till nearly dusk, un-

Setzer School (at Rowan County's Supplemental Education Center, Salisbury) was a "common school" in 1842 and may have earlier been an "old field school." Behavior was strictly supervised and lashes given for infractions of rules: ten for playing cards at school, "seven for telling lyes," seven for making swings and swinging on them, two for not saying "No Sir and Yes Sir or Yes Marm or No Marm."

doubtedly stretching both the children's attention span and the instructor's patience to the breaking point. The difficulty of dealing efficiently and effectively with the myriad of age and ability levels compounded the problem. Professor C. W. Smythe at a meeting of the State Education Association in 1860 aptly described the educator's plight: "There is no greater purgatory to which teachers can be sent than many of our common schools. . . . Children of every age, from lisping ABC darians, and those who are sent to get them out of their Mother's way, up to those bold youths who are exploring the mysteries of the Rule of Three or Cube Root, are huddled promiscuously together, each confounding the other and adding to the teacher's distraction who flutters from one to another like a bewildered bird."

The curriculum of most antebellum elementary schools offered little more than the rudiments of an "English Education": spelling, reading, writing, and arithmetic, and occasionally a smattering of grammar and geography. The books that superintendent Wiley authorized for use in the public schools included *Webster's Elementary Spelling Book*, known popularly as "Old Blue Back," *Davies' Primary Arithmetic*, *Bullion's English Grammar*, and *McNally's School Geography*, as well as his own *North Carolina Reader*. An interesting blend of grammar, literature, geography, and history, Wiley's book, much like promotional literature of more recent vintage, extolled the quality of life in the state and the character of its inhabitants. Like all readers of the period, it was intended to stimulate young scholars to read "with propriety and effect, to improve their language and sentiments, and to inculcate some of the most important principles of piety and virtue."

Few of North Carolina's rural schools had blackboards, much less the globes, diagrams, charts, and other apparatus commonly associated with primary education. The children generally sat on crude benches and worked in practice ledgers or on rough slates. The building, where one existed, was often no more than a converted barn or abandoned cabin with dirt floor, leaky roof, smoking chimney, and few windows for ventilation or light. Critics in both the legislature and the press were particularly distressed at the deplorable condition of many of the state's public schools, which they likened to everything from "Calcutta holes" to "a bear trap" and characterized as "utterly unfit for workshops" or "for civilized persons to inhabit."

Despite deficiencies in both facilities and instruction, schools were increasingly accepted as a necessary part of the nineteenth-century socialization process. Most Americans believed the very existence of the republic to be dependent on the continuous development of a virtuous, orderly, and knowledgeable citizenry. Thus, in addition to its educational role, the school was expected to train the nation's youth in political participation, law-abiding behavior, and responsible community membership. Whether or not institutionalized education ever had such a modulating effect, its impact was undeniably great. As editor William W. Holden suggested in 1857: "We can never forget . . . [t]he rude cabins in which we studied our lessons . . . The long and weary walks to school; the books we thumbed . . . The rivalry in spelling . . . The Master's looks . . . The rustic playground, and the mossy spring, by which, in the thick shade, we took our meals at noon; the ghosts we thought we saw, returning home late in the biting or the mellow eve."

Religion too was a vital part of nineteenth-century American life. Though only about half of the free adults in the state were members of an organized church, religious ideology, custom, and practice shaped North Carolina culture; and the local congregation, regardless of its denominational affiliation, formed the very core of the rural community.

Although many Carolinians of Scottish and Scotch-Irish descent clung staunchly to their Presbyterian heritage, approximately 80 percent of the churchmen in the state in 1860 were either Baptists or Methodists. Evangelical in their orientation and revivalistic in their approach, the predominant denominations directed their message toward the yeoman farmer and won an increasing number of Tar Heel converts, from Cape Hatteras to the Blue Ridge. While the Baptists confined their efforts largely to proselytizing within the white rural community, the Methodists' commitment to social reform attracted a considerable number of black Carolinians and "respectable" urban whites. The Episcopal church was strong in urban areas, and, because of the wealth and power of many of its adherents, was more influential throughout the state than its limited membership would suggest. The Society of Friends, or Quakers, was quite active in the central Piedmont, particularly in Guilford County, as were three major German denominations—Lutheran, Moravian, and Reformed Evangelical—centered primarily in Rowan and Forsyth. Disciples of Christ, Roman Catholics, Jews, and various other isolated groups completed an intricate religious mosaic, diverse at its fringes but cemented by the similarity of its European origins and the compatibility of its central tenets.

In addition to dictating both the form and content of religious practice, the nineteenth-century church demanded that its members adhere to a high standard of social and moral conduct. Thus, while yielding to civil authorities in matters of criminal justice, each denomination established and enforced its own rules of behavior. Offenses such as drunkenness, "disputing with a member," "neglecting Church service," or sexual immorality brought penalties ranging from censure to excommunication. Beyond "breaking the Sabbath" many churches disapproved of dancing, "fiddling," theatergoing, and "sports of pleasure" such as horse racing and tavern hopping. The

Old Bluff Presbyterian Church, near Wade, Cumberland County. A Highland Scots stronghold, sermons were preached in both English and Gaelic.

St. Joseph's Church, near McAdensville, Gaston County, is one of the earliest Catholic Churches in the state. It was built for Italian and Irish immigrants who worked in the gold mines.

Jamestown Meeting, High Point City Park, Guilford County, built by Richard Mendenhall.

Rehoboth Methodist Church, east of Pleasant Grove, Washington County, had a total membership of 160 blacks and whites in 1861.

Skewarkey Primitive Baptist Church, near Williamston, Martin County, shows the simplicity typical of the sect and contrasts with Bethel Baptist Church, Perquimans County, built by the prominent Skinner family.

Brown Marsh Presbyterian Church, near Clarkton, Bladen County. Thomas Sheridan, the free black builder, chalked his name on the ceiling. Many wooden markers, now badly worn, stand in the graveyard.

Before each communion service the members were quizzed on Scripture and dogma. Those who passed were given sacramental tokens admitting them to the service.

St. Andrew's Episcopal Church, near Woodleaf, Rowan County, shows a similar stark simplicity and integrity.

Society of Friends forbade its members to swear oaths, bear arms, and, most importantly in antebellum society, to own or hire slaves.

Church buildings in the rural South were generally constructed by the congregation itself. One member donated a small tract of land and others the building materials and furnishings. All shared in the labor and took pride in the structure that they created. A simple cabin served many a congregation until they could enlarge or replace it with a frame meetinghouse. Some were eventually able to erect a more substantial structure of stone or brick. The buildings of five of the churches that composed the Orange Presbytery in 1829, for example, were log, whereas twenty-four were frame and five were brick. Although the building costs of the four structures located in cities totaled $19,000, the average value of the thirty remaining country churches was approximately $63 apiece.

Most denominations were plagued by a severe shortage of ministers. Like those of teachers, clergymen's salaries were inadequate, rarely more than several hundred dollars per year. If they devoted their entire time to their pastorates, rural preachers were seldom able to support their families or fully pay their bills. Consequently many farmed or taught school to supplement their income. It was commonly said of Methodist circuit riders that they "preached by day and plowed by night," and in numerous cases it was true. How else could they be expected to deliver sermons at two to three different churches in a single day?

Neither Baptists nor Methodists required any formal education for the ministry; they placed more emphasis upon "the call" and a

Brown Marsh Church.

candidate's "public gift" than his knowledge of grammar or rhetoric. Presbyterians and Episcopalians, along with the three German denominations, however, maintained strict educational requirements. Though frequently the most learned and respected member of the community, many an antebellum clergyman was not above chewing, smoking, or drinking as hard as the staunchest members of the congregation. Occasionally a church even found it necessary to discipline the minister himself!

Because of the scarcity of qualified clergy and the time-consuming distances that they as well as their congregations were required to travel, country churches normally held services only once or twice a month. It was customary for entire families, from suckling infants

Zion Episcopal Church, near Washington, Beaufort County.

to graying patriarchs, to attend. When the preacher had arrived and the congregation had filed in, a deacon or elder known as the "precentor" rose to lead the singing. Hymnals as well as organs were rare, and it was the precentor's task not only to carry the tune, but also to "line out" every new or difficult hymn as it was being sung.

When the mood had been set, the sermon began. Given the rural clergyman's limited contact with his pastorate, he considered "teaching the scriptures" an essential part of every service. Utilizing a particularly weighty Biblical passage, he expounded upon such basic Christian themes as the "terrors of hell" or the "benevolence of God." Animated and compelling in his presentation, a particularly enthusiastic preacher often spoke for a couple of hours and characteristically elicited a vocal response of emphatic "amens" and exuberant "hallelujahs" from the inspired in the congregation.

Church services were more than an occasion to renew religious commitment; they were also a social event. Rural Carolinians gathered on the church grounds well before the meeting was to begin and lingered there long after the minister had departed. Many visited the graveyard where one or more loved ones were buried, while others earnestly discussed the day's sermon. Yet invariably the topic of conversation turned to more temporal matters, such as the outcome of a forthcoming horse race or the current price of tobacco. Everyone, regardless of age or gender, enjoyed the opportunity to meet with friends, share a laugh over a clever anecdote, and catch up on local gossip. While the more staid chatted quietly among themselves, the young at heart could be found carefully plotting a practical joke or preoccupied with the uncertain initial steps of courtship. Children wiled away the time playing tag in a nearby meadow or searching for salamanders in the adjacent creek. When at last the crowd broke up, it was common for "over half the congregation to go home with the others to eat late Sunday dinner."

Social Life

The lives of antebellum North Carolinians were not rigidly segmented into periods of work and play as are ours today. There were no timeclocks or two weeks of annual vacation. For the farmer, home and workplace were one and the same. Whether winter or summer, day or night, there was always something to be done. Many tasks such as weeding the fields or boiling lye soap could be onerous, while others like tracking a deer or picking wild blackberries involved less labor than fun. As for birthing a colt, building a chair, or baking fresh bread, the skilled effort required was amply rewarded by the pleasure of the accomplishment. Consequently it was within the context of their agricultural life-style, rather than outside of it, that most Tar Heels looked for their leisure as well as their livelihood.

This merging of occupation and avocation was clearly reflected in rural social life. Purely recreational events were few, but any gathering of a more practical nature, whether political, economic, or religious, was likely to take on a festive air. Election day, though ostensibly a serious occasion, was transformed into a time of fun and frolic. Crowds gathered early at the store or mill, which served as the local polling place, to be wooed by the rival candidates and to join in the merrymaking. Liquor flowed freely, and the political oration that marked the day was periodically interrupted by a horse race, a wrestling match, or a turkey shoot for which one of the politicians put up the prize. Inevitably, according to the *Raleigh Register*, "if some staid sober citizen was observed making his way to any spot where votes were to be taken," he was immediately surrounded by electioneers, "employing their talents, energies, and lungs . . . in order

A quilting party.

Dipping snuff, like smoking, was a convivial habit.

to gain his attention to their various claims, until the four points of the compass became . . . a matter of doubt and uncertainty." Though there might be some question as to whether the best man was elected, a good time was had by all.

The cooperative work and mutual assistance that characterized rural life also stimulated social interchange. A house raising was customary when a local couple married or a new family moved into the community. Yet it was difficult to determine who enjoyed it most, the thankful recipients or their generous friends. When sufficient timber had been cut and all the necessary materials collected at the site, the entire neighborhood turned out on the specified day. While the men, both young and old, worked on framing the house, the women prepared a huge midday meal. Not even the sound of the pounding hammers could compete with the hearty laughter and boisterous chatter that emanated from the scene. When at last the smells wafting from the open cooking fire overcame the hungry company and they stopped to eat, their eyes as well as their stomachs were treated to a veritable feast: smoked ham, fried chicken, roasted sweet potatoes, and buttered hominy—not to mention the garden vegetables, biscuits and gravy, thick molassas, and black coffee, strong and hot. And of course there were always sufficient freshly baked pies and cakes to allow everyone three or four slices apiece. After dinner the troupe labored to finish the roof before dark, leaving only the interior and siding for the new owners to complete. But the celebrating had only begun, for, as the last nail was driven, the fiddle was tuned. And the music and dancing, along with the drinking, lasted well into the night.

A similar combination of collective work and play could turn the most difficult or tedious task into a social occasion. Whether clearing new fields, building fences, or butchering beef, it was simpler and more enjoyable if a few neighbors could be mustered to help. Thus, while polite urban society might entertain with an afternoon tea, it was more common in rural Carolina to hold a quilting bee. The hostess provided the necessary material as well as the refreshments; her guests brought their needles and nimble fingers. And after several hours of lively conversation and deft needlework the group produced a durable quilt of attractive design and warm color.

Corn shuckings also served as an efficient means of preparing the crop to be milled and a good excuse to meet for some fellowship and fun. People came from miles around to partake of the lavish "shucking supper" as well as to join in the sport of the event. When almost everyone had arrived, the entire assemblage divided into rival teams. After situating themselves around a vast pile of the host's corn, the competition to determine which group could remove the leafy shucks from the most ears began. Before long someone struck up a familiar "corn song" and everybody chimed in on the chorus. A

(Opposite) Rockingham County entertainers. N.C. State Archives.

46

jug or two of brandy or whiskey circulated among the adults, as the tempo of both the shucking and the singing increased. To add spice, whoever came upon an ear with red kernels was allowed to kiss the person of his or her choice. Needless to say, many a clever young man ensured his success by arriving at the party with a red ear hidden in his pocket. The contest might continue until well past dark. Often it was followed by a spirited square dance, after which the crowd, with loud huzzahs for the victors, finally departed for home.

Weddings and funerals also occasioned large gatherings of family and friends. Marriage celebrations were eagerly awaited, and the festivities sometimes lasted several days or as long as the relatives could stay. Picnics and parties, hunts and hoedowns, suppers and sings, were climaxed by a day-long wedding feast. Even a wake, though fundamentally a solemn affair, could be transformed into a buoyant occasion, as the old men dealt with their grief by swapping the favorite yarns of the deceased or a graying woman contemplated aloud the potential represented by a new grandchild's life.

For many North Carolinians, however, the most exciting and important annual social occasion was principally a religious event. Since the Great Revival at the beginning of the nineteenth century, churchmen gathered during the late summer in the rural South and Midwest for several days of services and celebration known as "camp meetings." Intended to renew the zeal of believers and to gain new converts, many such convocations attracted several hundred to several thousand participants. They offered an inviting opportunity to interact with old friends and fellow Christians as well as a welcome respite from normal routine.

By 1830 the Methodist churches that composed the Lincoln Circuit in the western Piedmont had designated a wooded tract near Rock Spring in Lincoln County as the permanent site of their yearly camp meeting. Though the families who gathered there each August held their services in the open air, within a few years a large rectangular "arbor" was built to protect the assembly from the blazing midday sun and the frequent summer showers. Constructed of hand-hewn timbers, the open shelter remains on its original site shaded by a grove of sturdy oaks. A pine pulpit on the low platform at the west end of the historic structure stands silent watch over the rows of empty wooden pews. Ordinarily, with the exception of the shrill calls of the resident bird population or the gentle rustling of the trees in the wind, all is quiet.

A series of crude single-story row houses, known as "tents," surrounds the central structure forming a broad square. As their name suggests, these shedlike dwellings, built as temporary quarters for individual families during the annual meetings, gradually replaced the less permanent shelters employed by the earliest participants. Each consists of one or two rooms and a loft, the walls are unfinished

Arbor at Rock Springs Camp Ground, near Denver, Lincoln County.

48

The crudely built shacks of Rock Springs Camp Ground, called "tents," took their name from the original shelters used at camp meetings.

A similar campground is Tucker's Grove, also in Lincoln County.

An old-timer remembered that "the camp meetings at Rock Springs . . . had been the 'mating grounds' for that state for fifty years."

and unadorned, and the floors are hard clay covered with sawdust or straw. Nineteenth-century churchmen, caught up in the fervor and the fellowship of a vital religious experience were little concerned with material comfort. And the same is true today when Rock Springs Campground once again springs to life in late summer. For Methodist congregations from the surrounding region continue to gather at the rustic site in annual renewal of a tradition that has sustained them for over a century and a half.

Antebellum Carolinians came from far and wide to attend camp meetings, and some participated in as many as two or three in one season. On the day services were to begin all roads leading to the grounds were crowded with wagons and carts, groups on horseback, and entire families on foot. Everyone was there: young and old, rich and poor, black and white. The site bustled with animated activity, cheerful sounds, and colorful sights. Women chatted amicably as they set up housekeeping in adjacent dwellings and their children played together out front. A young girl sweeping the porch of her family's tent in her best dress returned the smile of the strapping lad who kept strolling proudly by in a pair of new, yet ill-fitted, boots. And various church officers scurried about to confer with their counterparts among the numerous congregations and to inform the heads of each household of the scheduled order of events.

The meetings typically continued from three to five days depending on the weather, the tenor of the assemblage, and the determination of the evangelists. Formal services could be held in the morning, the afternoon, or at night, yet there was always plenty of time in between for personal reflection, group Bible study, and casual socializing. Each day began with early morning prayer meetings and

49

"The whole area before the pulpit, and in the distant aisles of the forest, became one vast, surging sea of sound, as negroes and whites, slaves and freemen, saints and sinners, slave-holders, slave-hunters, slave-traders, ministers, elders, and laymen alike joined in the pulses of that mighty song. A flood of electrical excitement seemed to rise with it, as, with a voice of many waters, the rude chant went on."

Stowe, *Dred: A Tale of the Great Dismal Swamp.*

"Every August they would have a Big Meetin' and all the Niggers that had died durin' the year, they would preach them a funeral that day. They would build a big Bush Arbor an' Old Miss would give us this and that and we would cook it up and everybody would take dinner an' they would come for miles, all round in wagons an' car's an' spread a big dinner . . . I had my brogan shoes over my shoulder and had my dresses an' my pantalettes tied up with a string to keep 'em from getting dirty in the dust. I let my dress an' pantalettes down and put on my shoes when I got in sight of the meetin'."

Slave narrative of Catherine Beale, aged 91 in 1929.

was punctuated with family-style meals and impromptu musical performances. In fact, according to one knowledgeable observer, the site of an effectual camp meeting "ought to be almost continually vocal with psalms and hymns and spiritual songs, even the prayers should alternate with singings."

The principal services normally began with a hymn as the crowd gathered at the central arbor. Women and children filled most of the available seats while the overflow of men crouched at the end of a pew or stood under the surrounding eaves. Neither the wail of a discontented infant nor the whir of hand-held fans distracted the congregation as one after another of the several preachers who occupied the rostrum rose to speak. They might talk of God, of eternity, or of the judgment to come, alternately agitating and calming their listeners with the perils and promise of Christianity. At last, with the tension among the audience visibly apparent, the final orator brought his sermon to a powerful climax: "Aye! Ye are come as to a holiday pageant, bedecked in tinsel and costly raiment. I see before me the pride of beauty and youth; the middle-aged . . . the hoary hairs and decrepit limbs of age;—hustling each other in your haste—on one beated road—the way to death and judgment! Oh! Fools and Blind! Slow-worms, battening upon the damps and filth of this vile earth! Hugging your muck rakes while the glorious one proffers you the Crown of Life!" Many of the congregation were in tears. An old man exclaimed, "That Preaching!" Another blurted out a loud "Amen!" Several female voices broke into a familiar spiritual as the evangelist issued a call for the destitute to "come home" and be "washed in the blood of the Lamb!" And, as the "convicted" amid shouts of thanksgiving and cries of despair made their way to kneel at the "seeker's bench" in front of the pulpit, the ministers came down from the platform and moved through the crowd praying and shaking hands.

Emotional outbursts at such services were often accompanied by peculiar physical actions known collectively as "exercises": trembling, jerking, dancing, laughing, barking, and probably the most common, "falling down." Overcome by the passion of the moment, a victim would fall to the ground where "he might either become unconscious at once or he might lie where he fell groaning and praying until he was exhausted." At times only a few persons were seized by such an "exercise" while at others it might strike the entire congregation.

Because of the emotional excitement produced, many ministers actually opposed camp meetings, and the southern gentry remained somewhat reticent in their support. "Scoffers" were often present at revivals "to heckle the preacher or to steal among the fallen, feeling their pulse, or, in some cases, if there were any Negroes among the fallen, applying coals of fire to their feet." Drunkenness was always a problem, and in many cases enterprising entrepreneurs took advan-

At this mid-century camp meeting, tents were still the cloth shelters that gave their name to the later frame structures.

tage of the presence of the large crowds to sell liquor and produce from wagons or stands right on the campgrounds. Even organizers, such as James Jenkins, were concerned about the vulgar attitude that many participants assumed: "I am grieved to see so much labour and parade about eatables, and such extravagance in dress, I think we might do without pound-cake, preserves, and many other notions. . . . Many, I have no doubt, live much better, and dress much finer at camp meetings than they do at home; and this is one great reason why more good is not done; for while they come to serve tables, to eat, drink, and dress, the poor soul is little regarded, whereas it ought to be the all-engrossing care."

Although camp meetings were a popular recreational outlet for rural and urban Carolinians alike, for the most part, they retained their basic religious character. And, when it came time to return to the problems and prospects of everyday life, laymen and clergy alike did so with the vivid memory of their involvement in a moving communal experience, a deeper commitment to their Christian beliefs, and a renewed awareness of their own self-worth.

Town Life and Enterprise

North Carolina throughout the nineteenth century was economically, socially, and politically a rural state. At mid-century no more than 2.5 percent of the population could be considered urban and only the port city of Wilmington claimed as many as five thousand inhabitants. Yet, while "progressive" Carolinians bemoaned the state's lack of business centers to compare with Richmond or Charleston, the gradual process of urbanization, so apparent today, was clearly under way. The population of Raleigh doubled during the decade following the completion of the Raleigh and Gaston Railroad in 1840. And some twenty-five commercial and judicial centers throughout the state, such as Hendersonville, Salisbury, Warrenton, and Washington, were considered important enough in the federal census of 1860 to merit the appellation of "town."

The primary factor stimulating the growth of towns was trade. Consequently most were located at points convenient to water or overland transport. New Bern, the state's second largest city, was situated near the mouth of the Neuse and served as a principal market for the region drained by the river and its tributaries. Fayetteville, on the other hand, was located near the fall line of the Cape Fear and gained its prominence as a mercantile link between the coast and the Piedmont.

In most cases, important market centers became the seat of local government. But in the developing western region, because of the convenience of trading where legal matters could be handled as well, designation as the county seat was in itself often sufficient to create a town. Thus, many an urban settlement grew up around a rude, backcountry courthouse on a site selected not as a result of its relationship to established trade routes but its proximity to the geographic center of a newly formed county.

Although a few cities in the state, like Raleigh, were built according to a carefully devised plan, the majority developed haphazardly. Patterns of growth were shaped by a variety of natural and man-made features. The availability of water was critical to the siting of urban dwellings as was proximity to the courthouse or the town market for commercial buildings. The orientation of a particularly pleasing ridge line or stream had an impact on the direction and timing of expansion as did the desires of local entrepreneurs and speculators who owned the majority of the town lots.

The courthouse occupied a prominent site in almost every town: on the main square or at the head of the one street that comprised

(Opposite) Wilmington, New Hanover County, ca. 1853.

(Opposite) The location and layout of Raleigh were carefully deliberated and planned. The Capitol (1840) stands on the central of the original five squares delineated as open spaces in the city grid.

53

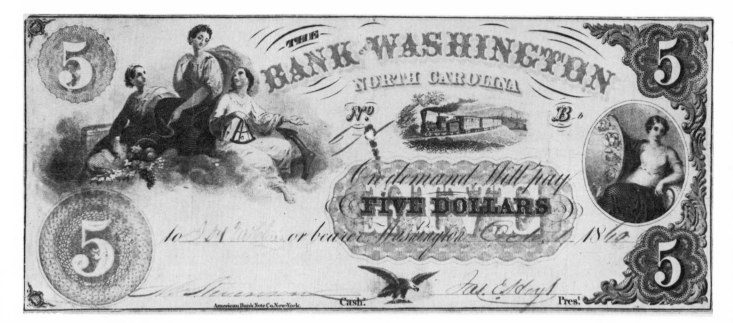

(Above) Bank of Washington, Beaufort County. Banks issued their own money. Currency courtesy Duke University Manuscript Department.

(Above right) When court was in session lawyers enjoyed the amenities of the Hoffman Hotel (1852), fronting the old courthouse square, Dallas, Gaston County. Now a private home, the hotel may be viewed from the street.

(Right) Wright's Tavern, Wentworth, Rockingham County, near the courthouse square. Photograph by Tommy Butler. N.C. State Archives. A log kitchen, servants' quarters, smoke- house, icehouse, stables, and store also stood on the lot in the 1850s.

the commercial district. Shops of local craftsmen were interspersed with stores of various sizes and types. Lawyers' offices, and that of a doctor or two, might well be found near the courthouse or scattered among the substantial residences that stood along the opposite end of the main street. In larger communities a bank was certain to dominate at least one corner of the busiest intersection, while a hotel, which was filled to overflowing during every "court week," stood on another.

Though largely economic and political in their origin and orientation, antebellum towns were important social and cultural centers as well. Urban churches were likely to be as architecturally impressive as the county courthouse and clearly reflected the interest as well as the affluence of their membership. Many towns could boast of the quality education offered by one or more private academies in addition to the civic awareness and moral uplift fostered by local chapters of various fraternal orders and benevolent societies. In a less formal vein, what could surpass the good food and fellowship of a midday meal at a popular tavern or the lively fun and frolic of a Saturday night at a back-street saloon?

Wright's Tavern Rates in 1821

Breakfast	.25
Dinner	.37½
Supper	.25
Lodging per night	.10
Whiskey & Brandy per ½ pt.	.10
West India Rum per ½ pt.	.20
New England Rum per ½ pt.	.12½
Holland Gin per ½ pt.	.15
Country Gin per ½ pt.	.15
Corn per gallon	.10
Fodder per Bundle	.03
Oats per Gallon	.10
Hay per hundred	$1.00

Butler, *A Courthouse Inn.*

County Government

Though ordinarily the centerpiece of the antebellum town, courthouses in North Carolina ranged from dilapidated wooden structures with decaying walls and crumbling chimneys to impressive monumental edifices of stone or brick. In the newly formed counties of the mountain region, a convenient tavern or converted barn might well serve to house the quarterly sessions of the county court until a suitable structure could be erected at the county seat. Farther east one was likely to find larger, more substantial court buildings, often with adjacent clerk's office and jail, which embodied the aura of permanence and stability that local authorities wished to project.

The magnificent Caswell County Courthouse in Yanceyville mirrored the growing wealth of the northern Piedmont that stemmed from the mid-nineteenth-century development of bright leaf tobacco. The imposing two-story structure, completed in 1861, was constructed of stuccoed brick on an elevated foundation of granite blocks. Heavy pilasters embellish the exterior facade of the building, and an octagonal cupola crowns the low hip roof. From the ornate Corinthian capitals above the main entrance, carved to depict tobacco leaves and ears of corn, to the coffered plaster ceiling of the elegant courtroom itself, the edifice is rich in architectural detail.

Prior to the Reconstruction era, the county court in Caswell and those throughout the state served as the administrative as well as judicial branch of local government. In addition to levying county

Caswell County Courthouse, completed 1861. The murder of Republican Senator John Stephens by the Ku Klux Klan in this building and Governor Holden's consequent suspension of habeas corpus led to his impeachment.

Caswell County Courthouse column, Yanceyville.

taxes, the court filled the majority of lucrative and influential county offices, including register of deeds, surveyor, treasurer, solicitor, coroner, overseer of roads, and superintendent of schools. It was the county court that licensed peddlers and retailers of "spiritous liquor," authorized the erection of public mills and toll bridges, bound out apprentices, and appointed guardians for orphans and the insane. Consequently the men who composed this multifunctional governing body exercised considerable control over the economic development of the county and the daily lives of its citizens.

Presiding over the county court were three to five justices of the peace. Commissioned by the governor on the recommendation of the local delegation to the state assembly, the justices of the peace were invariably selected from the county's economic and political elite. Customarily addressed as "Squire," the justices served for life or as long as they maintained their local residence. Each had the power to convene his own magistrate's court whenever necessary to "maintain, keep, and preserve the peace." As a magistrate the justice had the right to settle civil disputes not exceeding one hundred dollars and to collect various fines and forfeitures established by state law. The magistrate's criminal jurisdiction included the summary trial and punishment, up to thirty-nine lashes, of slaves charged with minor offenses as well as the arrest and interrogation of all suspected felons.

Four times a year the local justices gathered in Yanceyville to convene the county court. With power to summon grand and petit juries, the court had the authority to decide major civil actions and all criminal cases not punishable by death or dismemberment. However, because it was a common practice for the county court to deal exclusively with administrative matters during two of its quarterly sessions, it often took months for even the simplest case to come to trial.

Fortunately, North Carolina's system of justice was not totally dependent on the county court and the discretion of local magistrates. The state's superior courts had joint jurisdiction with the county courts in most civil and criminal matters as well as original jurisdiction in all felonies. Inasmuch as a superior court convened twice a year in every county, litigants had some choice as to where their cases would be heard. Judges for the superior court were elected by the combined vote of both houses of the state Assembly, and each rode a circuit of approximately twelve counties. Theoretically at least, they were less subject to local prejudices and pressures than the county justices of the peace. The same could be said of the three judges who composed the state supreme court and offered the confounded and the condemned a final avenue of appeal.

Punishment during the antebellum period was often discriminatory and generally quite severe. English common law, from which the American legal system was largely derived, prescribed a sentence of death for almost every significant crime. Even after 1855, when the state's criminal code was thoroughly revised and the number of capital offenses dramatically reduced, death by hanging remained the statutory penalty for seventeen major crimes. Obstructing railways, stealing slaves, or aiding in their escape, as well as murder, rape, sodomy, burglary, arson, and insurrection, all carried the death penalty. Branding or dismemberment was still prescribed for certain felonies; perjury, for example, was punished by the removal of an ear. Conviction for a misdemeanor might bring a number of lashes or an hour in the pillory along with a substantial fine and possibly even imprisonment.

Through most of the nineteenth century, justice was an overtly public affair. An execution invariably attracted a large audience, which not only transformed the event into a lurid spectacle but seemed to

Old Orange County Courthouse, Hillsborough, is one of the most attractive from this period. The members of Eagle Lodge laid the cornerstone in 1844.

The clerk's office (1831) in the county and market town of Jackson, Northampton County, housed all the court documents. A similar office (1833), also in brick for fire prevention, with brick flooring and a zinc roof, stands in Halifax, Halifax County.

Old Wilkes Jail, Wilkesboro, Wilkes County. N.C. State Archives. Here Tom Dula, the murderer, was imprisoned for two months before his lawyer, ex-Governor Vance, had his trial moved to Iredell County. He was hanged there but survives in a ballad.

"Oh, bow your head, Tom Dooley;
Oh, bow your head and cry;
You have killed poor Laury Foster
And you know you're bound to die."

Lines from an anonymous ballad.

Law offices from the antebellum period abound. They were usually one-room frame structures carefully built like this one, belonging to Governor Charles Manly in Pittsboro, Chatham County. Photograph by Tony Vaughn. N.C. State Archives.

lend the direct sanction of the community to the act of punishment itself. Yet even the most impervious of spectators gave a start when the trapdoor of the gallows dropped open and the victim's body writhed in final agony before falling limp in death. The example of what was to become of those who failed to conform to the dictates of society, as interpreted by the courts, was not lost on the crowd.

Communal scorn and public ridicule played a large part in other, less extreme penalties as well. Typically the county's stocks and whipping post were a prominent feature of the courthouse square. Not until mid-century did protests against the inhumane and offensive nature of such punishments become widespread. A report carried by the *Raleigh Register* in 1846 was characteristic of this carefully delimited, yet growing concern: "We have, this day, witnessed the most humiliating scene that has ever been exhibited before us. Two white men were, by order of the court, led to the public whipping post, there stripped and fastened, and lashed with nine and thirty, until their skin was rough with whelks and red with blood. We have never beheld a scene more degrading to the noble sentiments that should be nurtured and cultivated in the breast of every freeman. It makes us almost hate ourselves, to think that we are of their kind—yea, their fellow-citizens." But, in a statewide referendum later that year, North Carolinians overwhelmingly rejected the proposed state penitentiary that reformers were certain would prove the ideal form of social retribution.

For the litigants involved in the cases on the docket, "court week" could be a grueling experience. Yet for the community as a whole the periodic sessions of the county and superior courts were a lively time of camaraderie and commerce. Judges, lawyers, witnesses, jurors, and spectators all converged on the county seat. The courtroom was always packed and whether winter or summer "reeked of tobacco juice, whiskey, and sweating bodies." According to one young lawyer, there was "a continual fuss, a continual talking, so that the Court, the Council nor the jury cannot hear the testimony." The proceedings were repeatedly interrupted by distractions in the gallery or outside in the street.

Although the court itself was the primary attraction, agricultural societies chose this period to hold their fairs and political parties their district meetings. Enterprising merchants made the most of the occasion by offering special sales or hawking merchandise in the street. Roving musicians, jugglers, sleight-of-hand artists, and even tightrope walkers entertained the milling crowds by day while bands of traveling players filled the town hall every night. As long as it was not you, a close relative, or a good friend awaiting trial in the dank and dismal county jail, court week could be great fun.

Commercial Activity

Although the town's role as the seat of the county government pre-occupied its citizens during the periodic sessions of the county and superior courts, it was the municipality's function as a commercial center for the surrounding rural area that largely dictated the pattern of antebellum urban life. In North Carolina, coastal metropolis and backcountry village, regardless of size or sophistication, were still part of an agrarian society. Their development, in terms of both physical growth and available services, reflected the economic needs and aspirations of the entire region. Whether planter or craftsman's apprentice, merchant or farm laborer, the fortunes of town dweller and country folk were intrinsically intertwined. A good crop year meant increased sales, steady wages, prosperity, and possible expansion, whereas a poor yield raised the specter of high overhead, unemployment, growing debts, and impending decline.

This interdependent economic relationship was epitomized in the town market. There, whether daily, weekly, or just once or twice a month, in an open portion of the village square or within the boisterous confines of a municipal hall erected specifically for the purpose, the basic exchange of marketable goods took place. The wholesaler and the housewife dickered with agricultural producers, who offered everything from tobacco by the hogshead to flour by the sack, turpentine by the barrel to tallow by the tub. Planter and peddler alike selected from a variety of manufactured or imported products like Brazilian coffee and Cuban sugar, tenpenny nails and osnaburg cloth, which had been transported by the wagonload across the limited network of plank roadways and rutted cow paths that linked remote hamlets in the western Piedmont to the expansive market towns of the east.

Nowhere was the importance of the market and its attendant commerce more clearly evident than in Fayetteville. Well before its incorporation in the late eighteenth century, enterprising Scottish merchants had made the city a prominent center of inland trade. Here the antebellum farmer or country storekeeper had no need to halt his overloaded wagon in order to ask for directions when he arrived. The Market House, constructed in 1838 at the intersection of the four major thoroughfares leading into Fayetteville, was the focal point of the town.

The splendid two-story, brick structure of Georgian design is a classic blend of form and function. The ground level is an open arcade that served as the center of daily market activity. Stalls were set up in and around the building, while wagons filled with produce jammed the broad intersection. Yet Fayetteville's Market House was more than the nucleus of local commerce. The town hall on the second floor provided a seat for municipal government and a focus for com-

"I was born on a plantation near Fayetteville, North Carolina, and I belonged to J. B. Smith. . . . He owned about thirty slaves. When a slave was no good he was put on the auction block in Fayetteville and sold. The slave block stood in the center of the street, Fayetteville Street, where Ramsey and Gillespie Street came in."

Slave narrative of Sarah Louise Augustus.

Market House, Fayetteville, Cumberland County. N.C. State Archives.

The Liberty Row buildings, Fayetteville, Cumberland County, show two centuries of growth and change.

munity life and culture. On a given afternoon or evening, though the market was quiet, the building was still likely to be crowded with people attracted by a meeting of the town commission or a lyceum lecture. Even those who seldom had business there could not easily escape the impressive structure's subtle influence. The hourly chimes of the four-sided clock in the base of the cupola could be heard throughout the city, along with the mellow tone of the mighty bell that was rung four times each day: at breakfast (7:30 A.M.), dinner (1:00 P.M.), sundown, and the curfew hour (9:00 P.M.) imposed by the city fathers on slaves.

In addition to the curfew, the town commission was responsible for the formulation of all local ordinances and had the power to levy

A Yankee schoolteacher, George Hood, described Fayetteville in 1834: "The market too, you seldom see anything of consequence in it save Tobacco, Cotton and Slaves—the provision market is supplied from the country settlements. Some mornings they go to market and can get nothing—When I first came here Venison and wild Turkies was in the market—the season for those has passed and now we have fish. I board at a good boarding house—but still there is very little diversity—our breakfast is coffee, Corn & flour bread, Cold Ham—Fresh or Salt Shad and occasionally eggs.—Dinner, Bacon & greens, Shad, line of venison or Veal occasionally, Corn bread and Apple pie, Supper, Shad, Corn bread, hot biscuits, crisp, and coffee."

taxes on real estate, the sale of liquor, shows or exhibitions, and livestock that ran loose in the street. More democratic than the county court, the city government in the mid-nineteenth century was normally vested in a mayor and three to seven commissioners elected annually by the vote of all white male citizens. The commission was charged with maintaining public health, keeping the streets in repair, and establishing a night watch. In many larger cities, it was also responsible for recruiting a standing fire brigade and developing a municipal waterworks. Fayetteville by the 1850s could boast of two engine companies and a hook and ladder brigade composed entirely of slaves. Yet perhaps the most important prerogative that the town commission possessed was its power to establish and regulate the public market. Scales were erected and an official weigher appointed who augmented the municipal coffers by charging a fee for the service.

Antebellum Carolinians often traveled several days to bring their produce to market. Almost every night, particularly in the fall, the roadsides leading into Fayetteville and other substantial commercial centers were dotted with the campfires of those eager to be on hand when the trading started early the next morning. At sunrise the market came alive as teamsters jockeyed to get their wagons into the best positions and farm boys vied with merchants' apprentices setting up their inviting displays. The air was filled with the sounds of crowing roosters, barking canines, and shrill human voices already beginning to hawk their wares. And the pleasing sight of snow-white cotton, bright red apples, and golden ears of corn joined the rich smell of hay and manure as morning melded into day.

In eastern cities the faces one saw at the marketplace were as likely to be of dark complexion as they were of light. Many planters and merchants depended on trusted slaves to transport goods to

61

market, conduct their sale, and make any purchases required. Black traders, both slave and free, were also there to offer a wide range of merchandise obtained legitimately through their own labor or surreptitiously on the flourishing "black market." And the public market, where all other commodities were so readily exchanged, was normally the site at which those considered human chattel were auctioned as well. Few issues of the *Fayetteville Observer* were without such an announcement:

TRUSTEE'S SALE

On Tuesday of September Court next, at the Market House, in Fayetteville, in Pursuance of a Trust to me executed by James Sundy, dec'd, I shall sell at Auction

EIGHT LIKELY YOUNG NEGROES

Consisting of one Woman and the remainder Boys and Girls. These are remarkably likely, and of excellent character.

William Cade, Trustee

The town market, however, was by no means the sole location of commercial activity in antebellum cities. Stores and shops lined the principal streets near the market hall and around the courthouse square. Typically such retail outlets offered a broader selection of mechandise in terms of quality and sold in smaller quantities than could be purchased wholesale at the central market. While country storekeepers attempted to carry a complete range of products, their urban counterparts were becoming increasingly specialized, with dry goods shops, groceries, apothecaries, and hardware stores all competing for the business of town dweller and rural visitor alike.

Urban areas were a magnet for craftsmen as well. In addition to the blacksmiths and millers found in the countryside, almost every town could count carpenters, coopers, harness makers, cobblers, and tailors among the ranks of its mercantile community. Usually the services of at least one butcher, baker, printer, gunsmith, jeweler, milliner, and barber were available too. In fact, artisans and shopkeepers, along with their families and associates, were the very backbone of urban society. Living above their shops or in the unpretentious dwellings along the sidestreets of every Carolina town, these men and women, both black and white, provided the essential goods and services that attracted trade, stimulated cultural development, and brought the fledgling hamlet as well as the busy metropolis to life.

One of the state's best known and most competent craftsmen was a free black cabinetmaker named Thomas Day. Born in Virginia, he moved during the 1820s to Milton in Caswell County, which was rapidly becoming the center of the northern Piedmont's prosperous

62

The old Union Tavern, Milton, Caswell County, was converted by Thomas Day into a workshop and residence. A private home now, the shop may be seen from the street. Photograph by Walton Haywood. N.C. State Archives.

tobacco economy. Though he began his furniture-making business in a modest way, most likely on his parents' farm outside of town, within a few years he had established a thriving shop on Milton's main street. By mid-century, Day had purchased the Union Tavern, once the largest and finest in the area, and converted the handsome two-story brick structure into a commodious residence, convenient showroom, and functional workshop.

Despite their substantial contribution, free Negroes in antebellum North Carolina and elsewhere in the South were generally considered by whites to be an absolutely subordinate, though potentially dangerous, caste. In a society in which black skin was synonymous with servitude, the presence of free blacks, particularly those who even by white standards had to be judged a success, created a considerable dilemma. Their enterprise and ability contradicted the very assumption of inferiority upon which the entire system was based. As a result, they were denied full citizenship and restricted by various state and local regulations intended both to control and intimidate. In many larger cities, such as Fayetteville and Raleigh, where in 1860 free Negroes comprised almost 10 percent of the population,

Chair made by Thomas Day. Photograph by Walton Haywood. N.C. State Archives.

Milton Chronicle, 21 May 1858.

municipal ordinances required registration with the town clerk, the posting of a bond for good behavior, and even the display of a cloth arm badge marked "Free." The legislature in 1826 prohibited further immigration of free blacks into North Carolina, and the revised state constitution of 1835 deprived them of the vote. Although they retained the right of trial by jury throughout the period, free Negroes were never allowed to testify against whites.

This stifling atmosphere notwithstanding, Day and his family persevered. The quality of his work could not be overlooked. Many of the wealthy planters in the area as well as the citizens of Milton recognized his presence, regardless of his race, as a valuable asset. Day's services were in great demand. Working in solid walnut or mahogany veneer over local poplar and pine, his shop turned out elegant settees, ingenious extension tables, and elaborate marble-topped bureaus of unique design. Plantation owners depended on him to craft distinctive stairways, mantlepieces, and interior woodwork for their houses as well as rude coffins for their slaves. Townsmen contracted with him to custom build well-proportioned sideboards and graceful secretaries or simply purchased his practical wardrobes and sturdy bedsteads ready-made. As a result, Day prospered and, with the assistance of the young craftsmen, both slave and free, whom he trained to work in his shop, he became one of the most prolific furniture manufacturers in the state.

Thomas Day was exceptional, but not simply because he was able to develop his extraordinary skill and achieve a measure of success. The degree to which he and his family were accepted by the dominant white society was even more unusual than the esteem he was granted for his work. As early as 1830, when Day went back to Virginia to marry free black Aquilla Wilson, the white citizens of Milton successfully petitioned the state legislature for a special exemption from the law prohibiting her immigration. The Days were active members of the predominantly white Milton Presbyterian Church—for which his shop built the pews. Thomas was very likely one of the church's ruling elders because at least two of their session meetings were held in his home. In his business, Day could count among his regular customers the governor, David S. Reid, and several of the most prominent families in the state. And he was personally selected by the president of the university at Chapel Hill to execute the interior work for the splendid debating halls of the fashionable Philanthropic and Dialectic societies in the historic buildings known today as New East and New West.

But even a free black of Day's stature, who commanded wide acclaim and personal respect, could not escape the daily reality of prejudice and oppression. His entire family was acutely aware of the perverse character of southern society and sensitive to the anomalous nature of their position in it. Though he remained in Milton, the three children were sent north for their education, and Thomas and Aquilla longed for the time and place they might ultimately find both acceptance and contentment. Day's touching correspondence with his beloved daughter Mary Ann at Wilbraham Academy in Massachusetts in the early 1850s revealed his strong sense of isolation as well as the persistent hope that sustained him:

> You inquire how long before I leave & also observe you cant—se[e] how I have lived so long in Milton—I can tell you it will not be a verry great while before I hope to leave Milton—and I can also tell you I have long since learned to Enjoy my life in a higher circle than depending on human society for my comfort or happiness . . . No doubt my great concern at this time & will be is to get some sootable place for you and your Brothers—us all—to settle down—I want you to be in some place whare your turn of feelings & manners can be well met with associates—& I fully Expect to affect my purpose if I live long enough.

Unfortunately for Day, and countless other Carolinians, his dream was unattainable.

Society and Culture

Although not everyone shared equally in the pleasures or the problems of urban life, Carolinians of every station were attracted by the economic opportunity, the energetic spirit, and the cosmopolitan atmosphere of the antebellum town. Beaufort was no Boston, nor could Charlotte be compared with Charleston, the preeminent cultural center in the South. Even so, the budding urban character of such Tar Heel towns as Elizabeth City and Kinston, Tarboro and Henderson, not only stimulated more intensive commercial activity, but also increased social interaction and the liberating exchange of attitudes and ideas.

The elegant town houses of planter and merchant alike reflected their desire to be as much a part of the flourishing social life of the urban community as of its economic enterprise. Craftsmen, too, found more in the state's developing towns than a heightened demand for their various services. Not only did they enjoy more extensive contact with colleagues and peers than their counterparts in the surrounding rural area, but they also had a greater voice in municipal government and communal affairs. Even enslaved Tar Heels were likely to welcome the chance to dwell in the heady climate of a bustling port city or a vigorous inland town. Though it could mean separation from family and friends, as well as equally demeaning and demanding toil, an urban environment afforded the slave a freedom of

The Oval Ballroom, one of the Heritage Square historic buildings, Fayetteville, Cumberland County. Tradition holds that the Halliday family built the ballroom for their daughter's wedding.

The Joseph Bonner House, Bath, Beaufort County, overlooking Pamlico River. Bonner was a merchant who dealt in naval stores.

The Zebulon Latimer House (Wilmington, New Hanover County), Maxwell Chambers House (Salisbury, Rowan County), Roberts-Vaughan House (Murfreesboro, Hertford County), and John Vogler House (Salem, Forsyth County) show the wide variety of building styles and tastes of the urban merchant class. Liberty Hall, Kenansville, Duplin County, is the town house of a planter.

Purvis Chapel, Beaufort, Carteret County. Built by the Methodists in 1820, it takes its name from a visiting revivalist. First used by whites and blacks at both combined and separate services, it now belongs to the A.M.E. Zion Church. Another Methodist church of the period is in Wentworth, Rockingham County.

First Presbyterian Church, Fayetteville, Cumberland County, and Christ Church, Raleigh, Wake County, show the same prosperity.

movement and association unknown within the restrictive bounds of the tidewater plantation or the upland farm. Here too, as a result of an expanding market economy and an increasingly sophisticated and active press, one might learn more of a world beyond Carolina, where if Afro-Americans were unlikely to escape prejudice and oppression, at least they could be free.

Despite its multiple attractions, many of the very institutions that made the town an important social and cultural center served to reinforce the hierarchical precepts that split antebellum society apart. The urban church, like its rural equivalent, was a vital force uniting the diverse elements of the local community. Believers of all classes and colors gathered to worship simultaneously the same God under the same roof. But, regardless of their religious affinity, most congregations remained spatially segregated by race, sex, and wealth. In fact, church members often paid graduated prices according to location in order to "purchase" the right to occupy a particular pew. The composition of the numerous fraternal orders, mutual benefit societies, mechanics' associations, and other social organizations that sponsored the majority of the varied cultural and recreational activities associated with town life reflected similar socioeconomic distinctions. Though there were women's societies in New Bern, Fayetteville, Raleigh, and elsewhere, for the most part women and blacks, as well as propertyless or non-Christian whites, were excluded from membership.

To a great extent the enhanced educational opportunities available in an urban setting were also shaped by social and economic considerations. The principal means of progressing beyond parsing sentences and memorizing multiplication tables was the private academy, one or more of which were located in almost every town. These students refined their basic academic skills and were introduced to the classics of literature and philosophy. The most promising scholars, whose families could afford the expense, looked forward to continuing their education at one of the growing number of colleges in the state, while the remainder prepared themselves for more enlightened, if not more successful, careers in agriculture or commerce. Yet access to secondary education was not merely predicated on social status, ability to pay, or even race. Beyond the elementary level, female pupils found their educational prospects, like their vocational possibilities, circumscribed by their sex.

In essence, the only role available to women in nineteenth-century society was that of housewife and mother. As James B. Shepherd, a prominent state legislator and advocate of education, explained to the young ladies of Wake Forest Female Seminary in 1840, "To be economical as the head of a family—diligent in the employment of time—tasteful in the recreations of leisure hours— devoted wives—kind daughters—to render yourselves pleasant

Columbus Lodge (1838), Pittsboro, Chatham County. Another example of this type of structure is Eagle Lodge (1828), Hillsborough, Orange County. The masons' minute books reflect the concerns of the times: temperance, literature, statecraft, education, benevolence, and the social graces.

Burwell School, Hillsborough, Orange County. The excellence of its teaching made it an incubator of female educators. Schools all over the south were established by Mrs. Burwell's students.

Bedroom in the Burwell school. A student often brought a chest of drawers as well as a trunk to school.

friends, and benevolent in all relations of life are clearly the true interest and should be the sole object of your sex." Women did exercise considerable authority in certain additional areas in which their direct involvement was considered appropriate, such as church and charity work. But in general their participation in matters beyond the domestic sphere was limited to exerting influence on the decision-making process of men. Not only were they without a vote in political affairs, but apart from their husbands they had virtually no legal rights.

The rigid dichotomy of sexual roles was both reflected in and augmented by the educational process. Only a limited number of private academies accepted female students, and, even in those institutions established exclusively for women, instruction was more likely to be oriented toward developing "skill and grace in the home" than stimulating intellectual achievement. Elementary academic skills and practical household arts were supplemented by studies in novel reading, needlework, music, dancing, drawing, and painting. Yet, in spite of the popular conception of the woman's place in society, a few schools went beyond preparing young ladies to be "serviceable and pleasant companions" for their future husbands. In some instances,

the rigorous curriculum offered compared favorably with that available in the better male academies in the state.

One of the best and most widely known female academies in antebellum North Carolina was the Burwell School, located in the thriving court town of Hillsborough, in Orange County. The quality of the school's direction, along with its commitment "to cultivate in the highest degree [the] *moral* and intellectual powers" of its students, attracted scholars from as far away as Tallahassee, Florida, and Greensboro, Alabama, and secured the patronage of some of the most prominent families within the state. In accordance with accepted legal practice and social custom, the owner as well as the titular head of this remarkable institution was a male, the Reverend Robert A. Burwell. In fact, the school was originally conceived, painstakingly organized, and meticulously managed by his energetic and capable wife, Margaret Anna.

The Burwells first came to Hillsborough from Virginia in 1835 when Robert assumed the pastorate of the Presbyterian church. To help support their growing family on a minister's modest income, Mrs. Burwell began tutoring several local girls on an individual basis. As a result of what she perceived to be a compelling need, as well as her own interest in teaching, she gradually expanded the scope of her efforts. Within several years she was accepting boarding students in her home at the Presbyterian manse and had financed the construction of a frame classroom and refectory on the grounds.

Anna Burwell's school proved such a success that by 1848 her husband was able to purchase the property from his congregation and give up his pastorate to assist in its operation. An addition was added to the main building, which more than doubled its size and altered its orientation to overlook a beautiful sloping yard shaded by hardwood trees. And like the Burwells' own family, which eventually numbered twelve children, the school continued to grow and prosper. At its height the academy's enrollment was approximately thirty pupils per session, six or eight of whom lived with the Burwells at the school, while the remainder boarded "with some of the most respectable families in town."

The school year consisted of two terms of twenty weeks each with a break of six weeks at Christmas. Normally the annual schedule was coordinated with the various male academies in the Hillsborough area that brothers and cousins of the Burwell girls were likely to attend. Though not every girl expected to complete the four-year course of study offered at the school, the curriculum as a whole was comprehensive and difficult. In addition to standard subjects like grammar, geography, and history, the Burwells and their various assistants directed courses in mathematics, stressing both algebra and geometry; sciences, including botany, astronomy, and chemistry; and such provocative disciplines as moral and intellectual philosophy,

The Burwell School necessary house, down the path from the back door.

"evidences of christianity," and rhetoric. No wonder young Jane Bell's father, who recognized "that females and brains were not biologically incompatible," sent her to the school.

Mrs. Burwell placed great emphasis on writing and speaking English well. Her forte was literature, and she was particularly fond of requiring her scholars to parse the lengthy sentences of Milton's *Paradise Lost*. The girls were also expected to put their grammatical skills to practical use, for as Mary Pearce explained to a friend: "We have to write compositions every week, and I know you would feel sorry for me, if you knew how difficult it is for me, especially as we have to write something imaginative, and I am nearly exhausted of *subject*, *substance* and everything else."

The daily routine at the school began early with prayers and scripture recitations. Normally breakfast was a simple meal of bread, butter, and milk. "Divisions," or classes, followed at 9:00 A.M. and extended until 2:00 P.M., when the girls ate their main meal, prepared daily by the family's slave cook. Afternoons were devoted to the "ornamentals": piano, guitar, drawing, painting, and needlework as well as languages such as Latin, French, Spanish, and Italian. In the evening after a light supper, the Reverend Mr. Burwell led the girls in devotions, and Mrs. Burwell made sure she kissed each of them before going to bed for the night.

Saturdays were free. After writing a letter home the girls, properly chaperoned, could go "downstreet" to patronize Mrs. Vasseur's confectionery or the other shops in Hillsborough. "Authenticated callers" were also welcome, though the Reverend Mr. Burwell strictly prohibited casual visits of beaus from the neighboring academies. On Sunday mornings every girl went to church, and they were all required to attend catechism classes in the afternoon.

The last week of every session was devoted to review, and each year at the close of the spring term the school held its annual public examinations. The girls' copybooks, compositions, and varied works of fine and domestic art were put on display. Local luminaries were invited to question the girls concerning their studies, both individually and as a group, in order to evaluate their progress. Musical interludes punctuated the day, and the evening was entirely devoted to a gala "Soirée Musicale" at which the girls performed selections ranging from Strauss's "Tambour Polka" to Donizetti's *Don Pasquale*.

If Anna Burwell accepted the precept of the woman's place in nineteenth-century society, she refused to be inhibited by it. According to Burwell graduate Lavinia Cole, she "neglected no duty, kept the house beautifully, had the personal supervision of the thirty boarders, attended to their manners and morals, saw that their beds were properly made—was particular about their health—kept house, made her own bread, washed the dishes, with our assistance—taught six hours a day—was the mother of twelve beautifully clean, healthy,

Margaret Anna Robertson Burwell (1810–71). Courtesy Historic Hillsborough Commission.

70

and attractive children, dressed well always and entertained as much company as any other lady in the village."

It was not her intention to alter social attitudes toward women, but to encourage her girls to make the most of what latitude they were allowed. By her example as a successful administrator and mother, teacher and friend, she inspired a generation of young women to develop their own ability and intellect and to strive for excellence and achievement in their daily lives.

The formative influence of the Burwell and other private academies was significantly enhanced by the urban cultural milieu. Literary clubs and debating societies were in vogue. Though largely social in orientation, the implicit purpose of such organizations was to educate as well as entertain. In most sizable towns, a library association offered its subscribers access to a wide variety of reading material gathered in its private "reading room." The collection of the Raleigh Library Company, for example, included books, documents, maps, magazines, and a selection of sixty-seven newspapers, "one from every State in the Union and three printed in foreign languages." The local lyceum society annually sponsored a series of public lectures for the edification of its membership and the moral and intellectual "enlightenment" of the community as a whole. The periodic concerts and plays presented by amateur musical and theatrical groups offered merchant and mechanic alike a taste of the "fine arts."

The dramatic productions of the Thalian Association in Wilmington compared favorably with the "professional legitimate drama" that flourished in Richmond, Charleston, and New Orleans. Founded in 1788, the association's annual repertoire ranged from Shakespearean tragedy to contemporary comedy. The all-male company included such luminaries as Governor Edward B. Dudley and James S. Green, the treasurer of the Wilmington and Weldon Railroad, who was a star comedian. Often the Thalians engaged well-respected, professional actresses to take the female lead, though various members of the association appeared in female roles as well. William M. Green, who later became Bishop of Mississippi, was known for his "somewhat feminine" beauty and regularly won accolades for his performances as a heroine.

So popular were the Thalians in Wilmington that the city fathers prevailed on the state legislature to authorize fifty thousand dollars in municipal bonds to build a combined city hall and theater. The magnificent neoclassical structure was designed by New York architect John M. Trimble and executed by the finest local craftsmen, both slave and free. Constructed of stuccoed brick, the imposing two-story building is still in use: the front portion houses the city administration while the rear contains the beautifully renovated Thalian Hall.

On opening night in October 1858, the ornate auditorium was alive with the sights and sounds of actors and audience. Wilmington's

A former slave, John H. Jackson, remembered the building of Thalian Hall: "I was born in 1851, in the yard where my owner lived next door to the City Hall. I remember when they was finishin' up the City Hall. I also remember the foreman, Mr. James Walker, he was general manager. The overseer was Mr. Keen. I remember all the bricklayers; they all was colored. The man that plastered the City Hall was named George Price, he plastered it inside. The men that plastered the City Hall outside and put those colum's up in the front, their names was Robert Finey and William Finey, they both was colored. Jim Artis now was a contractor an' builder. He done a lot of work 'round Wilmington. Yes'm, they was slaves, mos' all the fine work 'round Wilmington was done by slaves. They called 'em artisans. None of 'em could read, but give 'em any plan an' they could foller it to the las' line."

Slave Narratives.

Thalian Hall (1858), Wilmington, New Hanover County, a combined theater and city hall. Photograph by Hugh Morton. N.C. State Archives.

social elite, elegantly garbed in velvet and silk, filled the orchestra level and lower balcony, while their servants crowded the gallery above. All eagerly awaited the initial performance of "The Honeymoon" by the professional company of G. F. Marchant, brought in for the occasion from Charleston. The glow of 188 gas burners highlighted the rococo proscenium arch that enclosed the stage and played on the fanciful vines and grapes that decorated the slender columns supporting the balcony floor. At last the drop curtain, which was painted with an idealized Greek scene, quivered and began to rise. And then as now, the hushed crowd was transported by the dramatist's insight and the players' craft to a different place and time.

Cockfighting and racing were popular
with everyone. N.C. State Archives.

Theater was only one of a variety of amusements that punctuated the daily routine in nineteenth-century towns. Gala subscription balls, formal suppers, and afternoon teas were held the year-round, but it was at more rustic pursuits that the average townsman was most likely to be found. Hoedowns were as suited to urban stables as to rural barns, particularly on a cool summer night. Cockfights were common in the spring and fall. And no Tar Heel town was complete without a racetrack, for horse racing was every Carolinian's favorite sport. Holidays such as the Fourth of July were typically celebrated with speeches, parades, games, and barbecues. And every few years a traveling circus, with its acrobats, animals, and exhibits of "natural curiosities," visited the larger communities in the state.

Despite the varied social and economic activity that added color and excitement to the urban tableau, the lives of antebellum townsmen differed little from those of their rural kinsmen and friends. Their days were spent in honest effort, whether at work or at play, and their nights in contemplation of the promise of tomorrow.

Ferry on the French Broad River. N.C.
State Archives.

Forces for Change

Although antebellum North Carolina lagged behind the nation as a whole in terms of social and economic development, by the middle of the nineteenth century there were ummistakable signs of an awakening in the "Rip Van Winkle" state. An expanding network of iron railways and wooden roadways linked the coast to the interior. The budding Tar Heel textile industry had grown as large as any in the South. State asylums for the deaf, dumb, and blind as well as for the insane demonstrated Carolinians' broadening commitment to humanitarian reform. Not even the debilitating impact of the Civil War could bring the progressive impulse to a halt. For out of the devastation and dislocation wrought by four years of conflict came increased economic diversity and positive social change.

Amidst the rising expectations and buoyant optimism of the Jacksonian era, emigration was the most critical problem facing the state. Every year thousands of energetic and capable Carolinians left their friends and farms to seek better opportunities in the West. A correspondent from Buncombe County reported to the *Western Carolinian* in 1827: "During the last four months the flow of emigration through Ashville has surpassed any thing of the kind the writer has ever witnessed. It was not uncommon to see eight, ten, or fifteen waggons, and carts, passing in a single day." Soil exhaustion, limited availability of new land, inadequate transport facilities, and lack of political and economic democracy plagued North Carolina during the 1830s, when the flow of emigrants reached its peak.

Legislators, planters, educators, and reformers all sought to reverse the trend by expanding opportunity within the state, though by and large the measures they proposed served only those Tar Heels who were free and white. The long-awaited North Carolina Convention in 1835 resulted in the ratification of a series of amendments aimed at liberalizing the state constitution. Henceforth, seats in the House of Commons would be apportioned solely on the basis of county population, and every white male taxpayer would be eligible to vote in statewide elections for both the lower house and the governorship. For the first time, however, free blacks were explicitly excluded from the electorate.

Ironically, North Carolinians within the government and without overwhelmingly approved of the forced emigration of a certain segment of the population on the grounds that it could not, or would not, fully assimilate. Thus the proud remnant of the Cherokee Nation was "removed" from the southwest corner of the state by federal troops

The Cherokee Indian Reservation, a tract of 63,000 acres in Swain, Jackson, and Haywood counties, was established for those members of the Eastern Band of the Cherokee Nation who had accepted state citizenship under the terms of the 1819 treaty and those who escaped forced removal in 1838.

in 1838. Although the tribe had been guaranteed "inviolable" rights to its homeland in treaty after treaty with the United States, the Indians' legitimate claims were superseded by what President Andrew Jackson considered to be the demands of "civilization." Approximately one-fifth of the eighteen thousand Cherokees driven from their towns and farms in Georgia, North Carolina, Alabama, and Tennessee died in military detention camps while awaiting departure or along the "Trail of Tears" on their way west. As a result of the removal, white Carolina gained over a thousand square miles of territory for new settlement. The funds garnered from the sale of these Cherokee lands enabled the state to embark on an aggressive program of "internal improvements."

The appearance of numerous journals devoted to improving farm methods and the quality of rural life, such as the *Farmer's Advocate*, *North Carolina Farmer*, and *Carolina Cultivator*, testified to an increasing interest in agricultural reform. Crop rotation, deep plowing, hillside terracing, better seed, improved implements, and the use of fertilizer were all promoted as means of increasing productivity and reducing soil exhaustion. A distinguished group of progressive planters organized the North Carolina Agricultural Society in 1852 with the goal of encouraging and coordinating local reform efforts throughout the state. The following year, the society held the first of its annual state fairs, offering cash prizes to attract a broad range of exhibitors. "Let it no longer be said," wrote the editor of the *Farmer's Journal*, "that the farmers of North Carolina are blind to their interests, and that they have no spirit of pride as regards the advancement of farming among them."

This sterling silver medal (almost twice actual size here) was created for the first North Carolina state fair. N.C. State Archives.

Handmade plow. N.C. State Archives.

The work of agricultural reformers notwithstanding, the welcome prosperity of the 1850s in Carolina and the nation as a whole was primarily the result of greater demand for agricultural products, higher market prices, and improved transportation. The total value of the state's crops mushroomed during the decade from $22,900,000 to $33,400,000, and land values rose by over 100 percent. Tobacco production almost tripled; that of cotton doubled; and, though the rate of increased output of corn during the ten-year period was less spectacular, the practical yellow grain remained North Carolina's leading crop in 1860 with a yield of over 300,000,000 bushels. It seemed to planters and politicians alike that their optimistic visions of collective progress coupled with personal wealth were on the verge of becoming a reality.

Despite North Carolina's considerable prewar economic growth, other states north and south were experiencing equal or greater development. Consequently, in a relative sense, most Tar Heels could be considered both backward and poor. Few yeomen fully accepted the concepts of "scientific" farming; crude methods and outmoded implements endured. Money was scarce and commerce was limited. Average income and standard of living were comparatively low. Markets and manufacturing in Carolina were as yet underdeveloped. Travel and transport through most of the state remained prohibitively expensive and frustratingly slow.

Transportation and Communication

From the colonial period onward, geographical barriers inhibited commercial development and intrastate cohesion. Although several major rivers dissect North Carolina's broad Coastal Plain, only the Cape Fear empties directly into the Atlantic. The southerly flow of the mighty Yadkin and Catawba rivers in the Piedmont, coupled with the attraction of superior ports at Charleston and Norfolk, directed agricultural producers to markets outside the state. In the west the mountains obstructed overland transport as well as social interchange with the east. As a consequence, most North Carolinians felt little more affinity with fellow Tar Heels beyond their own region than with their counterparts in neighboring states.

During the antebellum era, waterways served as the primary means of transport, and the advent of steam-powered vessels magnified their importance. Various schemes were advanced to increase access and improve navigability by building canals, dredging principal rivers, and cutting additional inlets through the Outer Banks. The National Republicans, and later the Whigs, projected a new entrance to Albemarle Sound as part of their nationwide plan for internal improvements, but the proposed passage was never opened.

Fayetteville, Cumberland County, early became a mercantile center because of its access to the port of Wilmington. Steamboats, barges, and all manner of craft plied the Cape Fear River.

Ocracoke Lighthouse (1828), oldest in the state.

The only viable entry for ocean shipping to North Carolina's extensive coastal sounds and the important rivers which flowed into them was Ocracoke Inlet. Even there deep-draft vessels had to contend with strong currents and dangerous shallows. A light marking the inlet was erected before the end of the eighteenth century, but it was rendered useless by a major shift in the channel. The federal government authorized the construction of a new lighthouse on Ocracoke Island in 1823.

Fashioned of brick and covered with mortar, the sixty-nine-foot conical tower is the oldest existing lighthouse in the state. The walls are five feet thick at the base, and a spiral staircase circles the interior to the top. Twelve trapezoidal lens panes are encased in the cast-iron dome. A valve lamp with reflectors originally served as the light source, though in 1860 it was replaced by a more powerful Franklin lamp.

Towering above the low dunes and the gnarled island vegetation, the structure was visible some fourteen miles at sea. Its height made it quite an attraction for the well-to-do planters who summered at Ocracoke. Asa Biggs recorded the thrill of climbing to the top to take in the view, for "from this may be seen all the Island and looking toward the sea the eye may spot any immensity." Islanders also congregated on the high ground of the keeper's quarters to wait out the worst of the frequent coastal storms.

Overland transportation was time-consuming and difficult. The state's roadways were for the most part ill marked and poorly maintained cart paths that became impassable in wet weather. The result, according to Governor John Morehead in 1842, was that it cost half the value of a farmer's crop "to transport the other [half] to market." Whether driving hogs or cattle on foot or traveling in heavily loaded wagons it was almost impossible for rural producers to cover more than ten to twenty miles per day.

Many believed the solution to North Carolina's transportation problem lay in an exciting new invention: the steam locomotive. The state government stimulated railway construction by purchasing substantial portions of stock in various private railroad companies chartered by the legislature, thereby underwriting much of the cost and assuming a large share of the risk. By 1840 the first two lines were complete. The Wilmington and Weldon Railroad, which stretched one hundred and sixty-one miles from Wilmington to the Roanoke River, was at the time the longest railway in the world. The Raleigh and Gaston line linked the capital city with the Roanoke as well, and with the existing rail connections from the river to Virginia's attractive markets.

Rail construction continued unabated until the outbreak of the Civil War, by which time approximately nine hundred miles of track had been laid in the state. Most important was the North Carolina Railroad, completed from Goldsboro via Raleigh to Charlotte in 1856. Although it followed a somewhat circuitous route through Hillsborough, Greensboro, and Salisbury—the respective homes of Governors William Graham, John Morehead, and John Ellis—it provided a functional link between east and west.

Speeding along at fifteen to twenty miles per hour, trains cut the cost of transporting freight in half. Lower transportation costs meant higher agricultural profits, and an increasing number of farmers were encouraged to produce a marketable surplus. Both intra- and interstate communication improved with faster travel and more frequent mail service. Railroads opened an entire range of new employment for both slave and free labor. Yet, as is often true with technological innovation, rail service proved most beneficial to those who were in the best position economically and politically to take advantage of it. At mid-century, though the state had incurred a debt of some nine million dollars to finance railway construction, over half of its citizens were still wholly dependent on the horse and wagon.

During the 1850s farmers and merchants agitated for the construction of a system of all-weather roads that would reduce the difficulty of transporting their goods to market or the nearest rail

Walker's Inn, Andrews, Cherokee County, was famed for its hospitality. "At William Walker's at Old Valleytown, was one of the very best houses in Western North Carolina, the bill for man and horse was fifty cents," one lawyer reported. Freel, *Our Heritage*. Frederick Olmsted found the house "unusually comfortable" but the food greasy: "what we call simple dishes, such as boiled rice and toast, were served soaking in a sauce of melted fat."

This inn and another at Blowing Rock, Watauga County, were stagecoach stops in the mountains. Kemp Battle remembered: "On our way back to Lenoir we spent the night in the only habitation in Blowing Rock, Mr. Sherrill being the owner. There were several gentlemen in the waiting-room. Our bedroom adjoined the waiting-room, with a bedquilt hung over the opening instead of a door. However, the food was good."

Governor John M. Morehead, influenced by his teachers David Caldwell and Archibald Murphey, urged or actually effected many of the internal improvements that took place at the end of the antebellum period. He supported railroad building; the educational system; industry; turnpikes; the founding of asylums for the deaf and dumb, blind, and insane; and a school for agriculture. He also advocated freedom, education, and the franchise for Negroes. Blandwood (1845), his home in Greensboro, Guilford County, survives as a tangible reminder of this "father of modern North Carolina."

connection. The legislature chartered numerous private companies to construct "plank roads" with the modest financial backing of the state. Because most of the stock in these ventures was purchased by individual farmers living along the proposed route, plank roads came to be known as "farmers' railroads."

Although such roads were built in almost every part of the state, Fayetteville served as a focal point for their development. Six plank roads converged at this thriving market center, the longest being the Fayetteville and Western, which ran 129 miles northwest through Salem to the Moravian town of Bethania, in Forsyth County.

Over five hundred miles of these wooden turnpikes were constructed in North Carolina, representing an investment of approximately a million dollars. Roadbeds eight to ten feet wide were surveyed and graded, then allowed to settle. Parallel rows of heavy timbers were laid lengthwise along the entire roadway and planks of heart pine, three to four inches thick, were placed across them. The structure was then covered with sand and the road was opened to traffic. According to a contemporary observer: "All classes profited, but the farmer gained most directly. Their peculiar merit was the diminution of friction, by which a horse was able to draw two or three times as great a load as he could on an ordinary road."

Travelers were charged a toll of one-half to four cents per mile depending on the number of horses in their team. In comparison to the railroads, most plank road companies were moderately profitable during their initial years. But, because of the rapid deterioration of the wooden planks, maintenance costs soon became prohibitive. Thus many roads closed as rapidly as they had appeared.

As improvements in transportation began breaking down the geographic isolation of North Carolinians, the concurrent expansion of journalism put them in closer touch with one another and the world beyond. Seventy-four newspapers, including eight dailies, were published in the state in 1860—over three times the number published forty years earlier. Because many were primarily intended to voice the concerns of political parties, they emphasized state, national, and foreign affairs rather than local news. After the telegraph was introduced in the state in 1848—the initial line running from Virginia through Raleigh and Fayetteville—items received "By Telegraph" soon began to dot the front page. One source estimated that by mid-century one in every three white males read a newspaper. The state's newspapers were supplemented by a broad range of almanacs, journals, and pamphlets dealing with every conceivable topic from religion to agriculture.

The steamboat, the locomotive, the telegraph—"internal improvements" and technological advances were everywhere apparent. The changes they wrought were cause for both wonder and concern. The editor of the *Raleigh Register* in 1850 voiced grave misgivings: "This is the age of high pressure . . . Men eat faster, drink faster, and talk faster, than they did in our younger days, and, in order to be consistent on all points, they die faster . . . It is to be feared that the invention of the lightning telegraph will give an additional go-ahead impulse to humanity, equal to that imparted by the rush of steam. If so, Progress only knows where we shall land." But, in reality, "Progress" was yet to have appreciable impact on the life-style of most North Carolinians. Despite the exciting advances in transportation and communication, few had more than limited contact with the outside world. Over a third of the state's population remained illiterate, and many Tar Heels still lived and died without leaving the county of their birth.

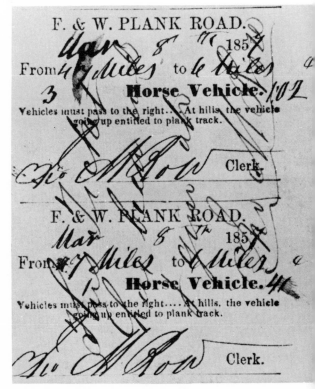

Passenger ticket for the Fayetteville and Western Plank Road, 129 miles in length, the longest in the world. "At hills, the vehicle going up is entitled to plank track." Weatherly, *The First Hundred Years of Historic Guilford.*

A letter from W. N. Tillinghast to his brother John, on 9 April 1850, reported: "The Plank Road is now finished to the Factory and Toll is now charged, the Country people do not seem to like it as much as they did before the toll gates were built . . . the land near town . . . has increased in value four or five fold."

Industry

Industry in antebellum North Carolina developed as an adjunct to agriculture. From mining to commercial fishing, turpentine to textiles, industrial enterprise was related to, and coordinated with, basic agrarian pursuits. Local planters not only provided the necessary capital, labor, and raw materials, but they also formed the principal market for the goods produced.

Although nineteenth-century Tar Heels mined limited quantities of iron and coal, it was gold that captivated the state's fancy. Begun on a part-time basis by Cabarrus and Mecklenburg county farmers, the gold-mining industry in North Carolina repeatedly employed some thirty thousand laborers and ranked second only to agriculture in economic importance at its height.

Gold was first discovered in the state in 1799 on John Reed's farm southeast of Concord, Cabarrus County. While fishing in the shallow waters of Little Meadow Creek, John's young son, Conrad, was attracted by a large yellow rock. Unaware of its value, the Reeds used the seventeen-pound stone as a doorstop. On a marketing trip to Fayetteville some three years later, John encountered a jeweler who promptly recognized the metal and purchased the nugget, worth several thousand dollars, for $3.50.

Reed soon discovered that he had been duped and came to realize the potential bonanza that he possessed. Along with three partners who supplied slave labor and tools, he scoured the creek bed each year in late summer after the crops had been put in and the stream had all but dried up. A growing number of nearby farmers began digging along their own creeks, and such seasonal placer mining continued throughout the region for over twenty years with considerable success. By 1824 the haphazard excavation on the Reed property alone had yielded an estimated hundred thousand dollars in gold.

During the late 1820s the budding industry boomed. Rich underground veins of gold were discovered in Mecklenburg County, and the corporations that controlled them brought in experienced European miners who employed the latest and most sophisticated mining techniques. John Reed, preferring to maintain a close-knit family operation, resisted the expensive transition to vein mining and the importation of outside workers, values, technology, and capital it entailed. But within a decade the younger members of the family had sunk several shafts at Reed Mine of up to ninety feet. After John Reed's death, the property changed hands several times until purchased in 1853 by the New York-based Reed Gold and Cooper Mining Company. The firm installed the most advanced processing equipment and sank fifteen separate shafts that were connected by a series of tunnels over five hundred feet in length. Despite its impressive effort the company went bankrupt, and, though the mine continued to lure a succession of new investors, it was never successfully operated again. It is now a state historic site.

The decline of the Reed mine mirrored the fate of the industry as a whole in North Carolina. When the first branch of the United States Mint opened at Charlotte in 1837, there were over fifty active gold mines in the state. But, with the discovery of rich and relatively accessible ore in California, few Tar Heel mines could continue to compete profitably. Although estimates of North Carolina's total gold production prior to the Civil War range from fifty to sixty-five million dollars, in 1860 there were only six operative mines in the state.

Manufacturing, even more than mining, reflected the economic dominance of agriculture in antebellum Carolina. The overwhelming majority of factories and mills were merely a subsidiary of their owners' principal agricultural interests. Based on the value of its product, distillation of turpentine was North Carolina's leading industry in 1860. Concentrated primarily in New Hanover, Bladen, and Cumberland counties, the turpentine industry yielded the state's only product with a substantial export market. Two-thirds of the turpentine produced in the United States came from North Carolina. Milling grain—largely corn and wheat—ranked as the second most important industry, followed in order by processing tobacco and sawing

Mint Museum of Art, Charlotte, Mecklenburg County. A branch of the United States Mint was established near the source of the gold in 1837 and now survives as a museum.

Gathering turpentine.

lumber. Though no other southern state could match the thirty-nine cotton textile factories operating in North Carolina, the value of their combined output placed that industry no better than fifth.

The Schenck-Warlick spinning mill, established in 1815 in Lincoln County, was the first textile factory opened in the state. Shortly thereafter, Joel Battle drew on the expertise of Scotsman Henry Donaldson to set up a similar mill on the Tar River near Rocky Mount. Although the original stone structure was destroyed during the Civil War, Rocky Mount Mill is operating today on the same site. By the mid-1850s Edwin Holt was producing his famous "Alamance Plaids" on steam-powered looms at his mill on Great Alamance Creek, yet North Carolina's textile industry as a whole had progressed only slightly beyond the domestic manufactures that it replaced.

Like most of the state's manufacturers, antebellum textile producers could not successfully compete in the national market. In fact, North Carolina was becoming less self-sufficient in terms of manufactured goods and more dependent on exchanging agricultural staples for items produced in the North. Ironically, improvements in the state's transportation facilities tended to inhibit rather than stimulate North Carolina's industrial development. For expanded waterways and railroads merely opened the state's isolated markets to increasing competition from the more efficient mills of New England.

The Schenck-Warlick Cotton Mill, no longer standing, was the first cotton mill in the state. Courtesy *A New Geography of North Carolina* and *The State*.

The second cotton mill in the state was the Rocky Mount Mill (Falls Road, N.C. #43 and #48), Nash County, seen in an 1863 picture. N.C. State Archives. The home of Benjamin D. Battle, the mill owner, now houses the company offices. None of the other pre-Civil War buildings survive.

Dorothea Dix's crusade for state care of the insane resulted in the establishment of mental hospitals in a number of states. Dix Hill in Raleigh, Wake County, crowned her efforts before the North Carolina legislature.

Her report had told the legislators how North Carolina cared for its insane: "In Granville County poor house is an unfortunate man, who for years has been chained to the floor of a wretched room; miserable and neglected, his now deformed and palsied limbs attest the severity of his sufferings through these cruel restraints; flesh and bone are crushed out of shape by the unyielding irons." Legislative Documents.

Josiah Turner, Jr., committed his wife, Sophia Devereux, to Dix Hill for morphine addiction. She found relief in writing poetry.

"I am leaving my grated window
Where I sat the long long day
And sorrowed and grieved for my children
Who are so far away.
. . . .
I can never forget the kindness
And the tender watchful care.
It was *all* that kept me hopeful
So my trial I could bear."

Courtesy Mary M. Barden, private collection.

Eumenian Hall (1849), Davidson College, Mecklenburg County, one of two debating halls.

Education and Reform

Nineteenth-century Americans trusted in the promise of social reform. To many, the expansive, individualistic attitude of the Jacksonian era signified a dangerous erosion of traditional values. The acquisitive forces unleashed by the growing market economy seemed to threaten the cohesion of the family, the community, and the young Republic itself. Continued social stability under such circumstances required the highest moral and ethical standards of every citizen. A growing segment of the population came to believe that the community at large should take direct action toward shaping individual character. Public schools were promoted as a means of instilling in every youngster a sense of morality and social order along with a knowledge of grammar and arithmetic. Benevolent societies were organized to combat vice and corruption as well as to alleviate the plight of the "worthy poor." Asylums and prisons were called for to "rehabilitate" social deviants by isolating them in a well-ordered environment until capable of coping with the pressures of a changing world.

The expanding interest in higher education both reflected and reinforced the impetus toward social reform. The University of North Carolina, chartered by the state legislature in 1789, had been damned by some as a "school for the rich." Yet during the nineteenth century "enlightened" administrators broadened its classical curriculum to include history, law, literature, modern languages, and natural sciences with such practical application as agricultural chemistry. David L. Swain, who became the president of the university in 1835 upon completing his term as state governor, "popularized" the institution by multiplying its enrollment and emphasizing the importance of training the state's brightest young men for careers in public service. During the same period, the principal religious denominations in North Carolina became actively involved in providing advanced study for "the humble student who would go out among the people and breathe into them the Soul of Education." Baptists, Methodists, Presbyterians, German Reformed, and Lutherans all established colleges for men. And, following the lead of the Moravians and the Quakers, most denominations sponsored similar schools for women. By 1860 "progressive" Tar Heels could boast of sixteen colleges, with a combined enrollment of over fifteen hundred, enhancing the knowledge and virtue of the citizenry in every section of the state.

The worthy social objectives behind the creation of such institutions did not necessarily ensure their success. Davidson College, in Mecklenburg County, for example, was founded in 1837 on the basis of a noble, yet abortive, experiment. Seeking a means by which "the cost of a Collegiate education. . . might be brought within the reach of many in our land, who could not otherwise obtain it," the churchmen of Concord Presbytery organized Davidson as a "Manual Labor

86

School." In exchange for a reduction in boarding fees, every student was required to perform three hours per day of "manual labor, either agricultural or mechanical." Those who had mastered a trade worked in the college blacksmith and carpenter shops while the remainder toiled on the school's farm. The faculty included a "steward" charged with supervising both the students' labor and the dining hall, which utilized most of the foodstuffs produced.

Although Davidson's founders were convinced that compulsory labor promised "the most happy results in training youth to virtuous and industrious habits," it soon proved as unprofitable for the administration as it was unpopular with the students. The majority of young men studying there had grown up working on family farms, and many considered their time misspent on similar endeavors at school. Procrastination and pranks abounded, for as one observer of student behavior suggested: "To cheat the overseer out of their labor, if practicable, was almost as much an instinct on the College farm, as it was on the cotton and rice plantations of the South, with the added zest that there was infinite fun in the thing, and it called for the exercise of superior adroitness." Wheels were mysteriously removed from the farm's wagons; tools were thrown under the chapel or buried in the woods; plows were purposely dulled and even broken. Within several years, despite the best efforts of the steward, the relative cost of the farming operation had become prohibitive, and enrollment had significantly declined. The trustees of the college were left with little alternative. In 1841 the democratic ideal of manual labor was abandoned for the standard classical curriculum suited to the sons of the "better" class.

Mount Pleasant Collegiate Institute, Cabarrus County, began as a Lutheran male academy in 1855, but soon became North Carolina College (now defunct). Antebellum buildings still stand on a hilltop overlooking the town.

Eumenian Hall debating room. Southern oratory was nurtured and refined to a high art in rooms like this. The University of North Carolina at Chapel Hill (Orange County) had equally elegant quarters for the Dialectic (Di) and Philanthropic (Phi) Societies, organized in 1795. The societies' valuable collections of books and portraits reflect their importance and their influence on student social and educational affairs. The Di Chamber (New West Building) is shown as part of the campus tour.

The "Manual Labor System" was not the only aspect of campus life influenced by the provocative vision of social improvement. Formal literary and debating societies provided a focus for educational as well as social activity at Davidson and other colleges throughout the state. Like their counterparts beyond the academic sphere, such organizations offered a forum for the lively discussion of topical issues—philosophical, political, social, or economic. The arguments, orations, and compositions presented not only gave members an opportunity to hone their polemical skills, but stimulated careful thought and continued concern about such controversial topics as social reform. Following the lead of more militant humanitarian movements like temperance, many collegiate groups went so far as to impose a rigid code of moral behavior on their membership. Both the Eumenean and the Philanthropic societies at Davidson established fines for fighting, swearing, intoxication, and "lying to the faculty." They even maintained "vigilance committees" specifically charged with reporting any such offense.

One anxious father, in Mocksville, Davie County, wrote his son, Albert C. McNeely, a list of rules to guide him in his college days: "Take care of your tongue, especially when excited be silent; Avoid night studies after 10 o'clock; Exercise should be uniform as the sun; always before meals, if you can; Join no combination to resist authority."

Richmond Temperance and Literary Society Hall, Spring Hill near Wagram, Scotland County. The down-turned wine glass on a book forms the wooden finial.

It was not uncommon for benevolent societies outside the collegiate environment to mix educational and social motives as well. Such was the case in Spring Hill, near Wagram in what is now Scotland County, where a group of upper- and middle-class farmers gathered to form the Richmond Temperance and Literary Society in 1855. Their goals were forthright and their concerns real, as their constitution vividly suggests:

> We a portion of the citizens of this community being convinced of the deadly influence that intemperance is now exerting over the morality of our country, and plainly seeing the ravages that it is daily making in our midst, burying the brightest talents in an untimely grave, levelling man the noblest work of God's creation with the beasts of the field, staying the hand of everything that has for its object the advancement of virtue and religion; do ordain and establish . . . this Society . . . its objects being uncompromising hostility to intemperance and an untiring zeal for the advancement of literature.

The temperance movement arrived in North Carolina in the 1820s in conjunction with demands for a wide range of humanitarian reforms. By mid-century some 12,000 Tar Heels had taken the temperance pledge to "neither make, sell, buy, nor use as a beverage any intoxicating drink whatever." The Richmond Society was more active than most, meeting every other Saturday—2:00 P.M. in winter, 3:00 P.M. in summer. The bylaws were strictly adhered to, including the fine for absence of twenty-five cents. Meetings were alternately devoted to the presentation of a member's literary composition and to open debate. After singing a rousing stanza or two of "Round the Temperance Standard Rally" or "The Teetotalers are Coming," the twenty or so members and guests might begin a thoughtful discussion of an esoteric topic like "Which is most sought after, Wealth or Honor" or a more volatile debate over a timely question such as "Has the Insurrection at Harper's Ferry been a Benefit to the Union?" Though it might never match the garish excitement of a barroom bash, a temperance meeting, by all accounts, could be a truly edifying experience.

War and Reconstruction

The Civil War ravaged North Carolina—both its families and its farms. Forty thousand men, more than from any other southern state, were lost in their prime. Thousands more were scarred and damaged, left with only their courage and their pride. Millions of dollars in local, state, and Confederate revenue were spent for naught as well. Investments, savings, loans, and currency, all were ren-

James F. Cain, a student of Chapel Hill, wrote to his sister, Mrs. Tod Caldwell, in 1849: "There is no news in H[illsborough]—but that Mrs. Burwell's School is increasing and Presbyterian fanaticism raging at its highest pitch. They are exulting, proclaiming aloud, with their hands raised to Heaven, for the 'success of the Temperance cause' and the downfall of all the grogeries in H[illsborough] —every institution of the kind in the place has been refused license to retail spirituous liquors—."

Dead Civil War soldier. N.C. State Archives.

Union scout.

Harper House, Bentonville Battlefield, Johnston County. N.C. State Archives.

Civil War actions involved Fort Fisher, New Hanover County, and Fort Macon, Carteret County. Archeological exhibits and earthworks remain at the first, while a complete restoration may be seen at the second.

dered worthless with no hope of reparation. Countless banks, mills, stores, and schools were closed forever. Blighted crops, empty barnyards, fallen fences, and broken dreams, all had to be dealt with in the midst of defeat.

More threatening still to conservative whites was the specter of social revolution. Three hundred and fifty thousand black Carolinians, over a third of the state's population, experienced the joy of "Jubilee." For now the enslaved would be free—to rejoin their scattered families, to take up vacant farm lands, to compete for available jobs, and to demand their civil rights. Indeed, North Carolina would never be the same.

While a hundred thousand Tar Heels marched off to battle, nine times that number remained home. Faced with scarcities, exorbitant prices, and depreciating currency, farm wives and plantation mistresses, old men and small children, free blacks and domestic servants, all strove to make ends meet. Houses were stripped of draperies and carpets to provide clothing and shelter for Carolina's troops. Parched corn was substituted for coffee, and spinning wheels once more competed with power looms. Yet opportunistic farmers and unscrupulous blockade runners continued to sell their goods at the highest prices the market would bear. Bacon jumped from 33 cents to $7.50 per pound, wheat went from $3 to $50 a bushel, and coffee was selling at $100 per pound.

Although the day-to-day hardships on the homefront brought frustration and care, the threat of nearby fighting prompted unnerving thoughts and fears. Catherine Edmondston of Halifax described her feelings poetically in 1863:

Heard distinctly the report of two heavy guns in the direction of Weldon. The boom was unmistakable . . . What a sad solemn sound it is! The deep toned roar! This note of horrid war which comes booming over the peaceful fields & through the still quiet swamps & woods, awakening echoes which until now have slept to all save peaceful sounds. It makes the blood tingle through ones veins and brings the war home to our very thresholds.

John and Amy Harper of Bentonville in Johnston County knew that feeling well. For in March 1865 the largest land battle ever fought in North Carolina took place before their doorstep. Located behind the Union line, the Harper home was commandeered for a field hospital. Colonel William Hamilton of the Ohio cavalry described the bloody sight: "A dozen surgeons and attendants in their shirt sleeves stood at the rude benches cutting off arms and legs and throwing them out of the window where they lay scattered on the grass. The legs of the infantrymen could be distinguished from those of the cavalry by the size of their calves, as the march of 1000 miles had increased the size of one and diminished the size of the other."

With the brutal horror of warfare thrust unexpectedly upon them, the Harpers did what they could to relieve the suffering, acting as "nurses, surgeons, commissaries, chaplins and undertakers" for the dead and dying.

The war presented a particular dilemma for enslaved Carolinians. With rumors rampant and conflicting reports of freedom and reenslavement circulating on plantations throughout the state, it was extremely hard to determine an appropriate course of action. Some remained on their owner's land trusting in the possibility of "inheriting" a portion of it for themselves. Others seized the opportunity to run away, often joining the thousands of "contrabands" attracted by the relative security represented by the Union army. Their numbers became such a logistical problem that camps were established to house the new "freedmen" at various locations in the occupied eastern portion of the state. Volunteers from the northern states assisted in setting up schools, clinics, and other necessary services, while the freedmen themselves were assigned small tracts of land on which they could eke out an existence.

The wartime experience gained in the contraband camps led in 1865 to the establishment of a federally funded Freedmen's Bureau, charged with easing the transition from former slave to free citizen. The bureau operated throughout the South, with regional offices in every state. The headquarters for North Carolina were located in the impressive, Greek Revival main building of what is now Peace College. Despite the Bureau's efforts to assist freedmen in finding employment, negotiating fair contracts, and settling legal disputes, black Carolinians remained at a distinct political, economic, and social disadvantage. The state's conservative leadership marshaled the en-

An ex-slave remembered the Freedmen's Bureau: "When we lef de white folks we had nothing to eat. De niggers wait there at de bureau and they give 'em hard tack, white potatoes, and saltpeter meat. Our white folks give us good things to eat, and I cried everyday at 12 o'clock to go home . . . I would say 'Papa le's go home, I want to go home. I don't like this sumpin' to eat.' He would say, 'Don't cry, honey, le's stay here, dey will sen' you to school.'"

Slave narrative of Sarah Harris.

Peace College. Built as a school for girls, it served as a Civil War Hospital, the headquarters of the Freedmen's Bureau, and then once more as a school. Charles L. Smith, *History of Education in North Carolina* (Washington, D.C., 1888).

Dr. W. M. McPheeters wrote in 1862: "The Peace Institute here which is used as a Conf. hospital is an admirable institution & had it been erected for hospital purposes could not have been better adapted to that purpose. It will accomodate 300 patients well & has at present 199 & is under the charge of a Dr. Hill an Assistant Surgeon."

trenched racism and staunch solidarity of the white population in order to thwart black achievement and to maintain control.

As a consequence, postwar Reconstruction in North Carolina actually resulted in less change than most Tar Heels either hoped, or feared, would take place. Political and economic gains by blacks were, for the most part, temporary and slight. The majority of ex-slaves in the state became sharecroppers and were soon bound to large landowners by a tangled web of intimidation and debt. "Rural" and "self-sufficient" remained the appropriate description of the majority of whites. Land values had declined and participation in the market economy increased, but the small farmer was actually in the best position to weather the economic dislocations with which the southern economy was faced. There were signs of a new era, though their impact was yet to be felt. In tobacco and textiles, new technology, ready capital, and cheap labor were soon to have revolutionary effects.

Bibliography

Printed Sources

Anderson, Jean B. "A Community of Men and Mills." *Eno Journal*, March 1980.

———. "Piedmont Plantation." Report, N.C. Division of Archives and History, 1977.

Atherton, Lewis E. *The Southern Country Store, 1800–1860*. Baton Rouge, 1949.

Barfield, Rodney. *Thomas Day, Cabinetmaker*. Raleigh, 1975.

Battle, Kemp P. *Memories of an Old-Time Tar Heel*. Chapel Hill, 1945.

Blassingame, John W. *The Slave Community: Plantation Life in the Antebellum South*. New York, 1972.

Bruce, Dickson D., Jr. *And They All Sang Hallelujah*. Knoxville, Tenn., 1946.

Butler, Lindley S. *A Courthouse Inn and Its Proprietors*. Wentworth, N.C., 1973.

Campbell, Wanda S. *Brown Marsh Presbyterian Church, Bladen County, North Carolina, Historical Records*. Elizabethtown, N.C., 1970.

Carter, Samuel, III. *Cherokee Sunset: A Nation Betrayed*. Garden City, N.Y., 1976.

Cashion, Jerry. "Fort Butler and the Cherokee Indian Removal from North Carolina." Report, Department of Archives and History, 1970.

Cathey, Cornelius O. *Agricultural Developments in North Carolina, 1783–1860*. James Sprunt Studies in History and Political Science. Chapel Hill, 1956.

Coon, Charles L. *North Carolina Schools and Academies, 1790–1840*. Raleigh, 1915.

Cross, Jerry L. "Historical Research Report for the Harper House, Bentonville, North Carolina." Report, Division of Archives and History, 1975.

Edmondston, Catherine Ann Devereux. *"Journal of a Secesh Lady."* Edited by Beth G. Crabtree and James W. Patton. Raleigh, 1979.

Edmunds, Mary L. R. *Governor Morehead's Blandwood and the Family who Lived There*. Greensboro, 1976.

Epstein, Dena J. *Sinful Tunes and Spirituals: Black Folk Music to the Civil War*. Urbana, 1977.

Franklin, John Hope. *The Free Negro in North Carolina, 1790–1860*. Chapel Hill, 1943.

Freel, Margaret W. *Our Heritage: The People of Cherokee County, North Carolina*. Asheville, 1956.

Gutman, Herbert G. *The Black Family in Slavery and Freedom, 1750–1925*. New York, 1976.

Hawkins, William G. *Lunsford Lane: Or, Another Helper from North Carolina*. Boston, 1863.

Hodges, J. E. *A History of Balls Creek Camp Ground, 1853–1929*. Maiden, N.C., 1929.

Hunter, Robert, Jr. *Quebec to Carolina in 1785–1786, Being the Travel Diary and Observations of Robert Hunter, Jr., A Young Merchant of London*. Edited by Louis B. Wright and Marion Tinling. San Marino, Calif., 1943.

Jackson, George P. *Spiritual Folksongs of Early America*. Locust Valley, N.Y., 1953.

Johnson, Guion G. *Ante-Bellum North Carolina: A Social History*. Chapel Hill, 1937.

Knapp, Richard F. *Golden Promise in the Piedmont: The Story of John Reed's Mine*. Raleigh, 1975.

Knight, Edgar W. *Public School Education in North Carolina*. Boston, 1916.

Konkle, Burton A. *John Motley Morehead and the Development of North Carolina*. Philadelphia, 1922.

Lefler, Hugh T., and Newsome, Albert R. *North Carolina: The History of a Southern State*. 3d ed. Chapel Hill, 1973.

Lemmon, Sarah McC., ed. *The Pettigrew Papers*. Vol. 1, 1685–1818. Raleigh, 1971.

———. "Plantation Life at Lake Phelps before the Civil War." A paper presented at the Edenton Symposium, Division of Archives and History, 1976.

Lossing, Benson J. *The Pictorial Fieldbook of the Revolution*. New York 1860.

McDaniel, George. "Stagville: Kin and Community." Report, Division of Archives and History, 1977.

Menius, Arthur. "The Bennett Place." Report, Division of Archives and History, 1979.

Marshall, Helen E. *Dorothea Dix*. Chapel Hill, 1937.

Muse, Amy. *The Story of the Methodists in the Port of Beaufort*. New Bern, N.C., 1941.

Olmsted, Frederick L. *The Cotton Kingdom*. New York, 1953.

Owens, Leslie H. *This Species of Property: Slave Life and Culture in the Old South*. New York, 1976.

Owsley, Frank L. *Plain Folk of the Old South*. Baton Rouge, 1949.

The Poetical Works of George M. Horton, the Colored Bard of North Carolina. Hillsborough, N.C., 1845.

Powell, William S. *When the Past Refused to Die: A History of Caswell County*. Durham, 1977.

Robinson, Blackwell P., ed. *The North Carolina Guide*. Chapel Hill, 1955.

Rothman, David J. *The Discovery of the Asylum: Social Order and Disorder in the New Republic*. Boston, 1971.

Rulfs, Donald J. "The Professional Theater in Wilmington." *North Carolina Historical Review* 28 (1951): 119–36.

Shaw, Cornelia R. *Davidson College*. New York, 1923.

Slave Narratives: A Folk History of Slavery in the United States from Interviews with Former Slaves. Typewritten records prepared by the Federal Writers' Project, Works Progress Administration. Washington, D.C., 1941. Vol. 11 (North Carolina). Microfiche. William R. Perkins Library, Duke University.

Spruill, Julia Cherry. *Women's Life and Work in the Southern Colonies*. Chapel Hill, 1938.

Stowe, Harriet B. *Dred: A Tale of the Great Dismal Swamp*. Boston, 1856.

Studebaker, Robert B. *History of Eagle Lodge*. Chapel Hill, n.d.

Tarlton, William S. "Somerset Place and Its Restoration." Report, Division of State Parks. 1954.

The Thalian Association of Wilmington, North Carolina, with Sketches of Many of Its Members by a Member of the Association. Wilmington, 1871.

Wall, Bennett H. "Ebenezer Pettigrew: An Economic Study of an Ante-Bellum Planter." Ph.D. dissertation, University of North Carolina at Chapel Hill, 1946.

Weatherly, Andrew Earl. *The First Hundred Years of Historic Guilford, 1771–1871*. Greensboro, 1972.

West, John F. *The Ballad of Tom Dula*. Durham, n.d.

Wilson, Peter M. *Southern Exposure*. Chapel Hill, 1927.

Manuscript Sources

Manuscript Department, William R. Perkins Library, Duke University, Durham.

James Bennitt Papers.
Campbell Family Papers.
Joseph F. Fowler Papers.
George Hood Papers.
Thomas C. McNeeley Papers.
Alexander McPheeters Papers.
Officers' and Soldiers' Miscellaneous Letters, 1861, Confederate States of America, Archives, Army, Miscellany.
Tillinghast Family Papers.
John Wilson Papers.
John Wilson and Richard T. Smith Account Book.

North Carolina State Archives, Raleigh.

Legislative Documents, Session 1848–1849, House Document No. 2. "A Memorial Soliciting a State Hospital for the Protection and Care of the Insane."
Michaux-Randolph Papers: "A Concise Account of the Rise of Camp Meetings."

Southern Historical Collection, Louis R. Wilson Library, University of North Carolina, Chapel Hill.

Asa Biggs Papers.
Cameron Family Papers.
Tod R. Caldwell Papers.

Newspapers and Magazines

Greensboro Daily News (special historical edition), 29 May 1971.
Hillsborough Recorder.
Milton Chronicle.
The State Magazine.

Acknowledgments

The efforts of many persons have gone into this work. The suggestions that resulted from our public appeal for information as well as the knowledge of experts in many areas have enhanced the quality of this book and facilitated its production. Volunteers who led us to privately owned sites and out-of-the-way places have added materially to the gathering and scope of the information in this volume. To all these contributors the staff is sincerely grateful. We especially wish to thank Mary M. Barden, Rodney Barfield, Larry Bennett, Catherine Bishir, Jerry Cashion, Jeffrey Crow, Margaret DeRosset, Mary Clare Engstrom, Gayle Fripp, Kirk Fuller, Brent Glass, Renee Gledhill Earley, Alice Henderson, Davyd Hood, Sal Levi, Ruth Little-Stokes, Bill Murphy, Mary E. Ragsdale, Joseph Reckford, Marguerite Schumann, Michael Southern, Carol Spears, Greer Suttlemyre, and Susan Walker.

The staffs of various institutions have also aided our research: the Manuscript, Newspapers and Microforms, and Rare Books departments of the William R. Perkins Library, Duke University; the North Carolina Collection and the Southern Historical Collection of the Louis R. Wilson Library, University of North Carolina at Chapel Hill; and the Archeology and Historic Preservation, Archives and Records, Historic Sites, Survey and Planning, and the Technical Services sections of the Division of Archives and History, North Carolina Department of Cultural Resources. To all of them it is a pleasure to acknowledge our indebtedness and thanks.

Drawings not otherwise credited are from the following sources:

Ballou's Pictorial Drawing-Room Companion.

Billings, E. R. *Tobacco: Its History, Varieties, Culture, Manufacture, and Commerce.* Hartford, 1875.

Butterworth, Benjamin. *The Growth of Industrial Arts.* Washington, D.C., 1892.

Colyer, Vincent. *Report of the Services Rendered by the Freed People in North Carolina.* New York, 1864.

Gleason's Pictorial Drawing-Room Companion.

Gorham, B. Weed. *Camp Meeting Manual: A Practical Book for the Camp Ground.* Boston, 1854.

Harper's Weekly and *Monthly.*

1000 Quaint Cuts (New York, 1973 reprint).

1 Cherokee County

Walker's Inn, *Andrews*.

Swain County

Cherokee Indian Reservation.
Pioneer Farmstead, *U.S. #441, Great
Smoky Mountains National Park,
near Cherokee.*

Jackson County

Cherokee Indian Reservation.

Haywood County

Cherokee Indian Reservation.

Henderson County

Woodfields Inn, *Flat Rock*.

Wilkes County

Old County Jail, *Wilkesboro*.

Lincoln County

Rock Springs Camp Ground, *near
Denver.*
Tucker's Grove Camp Ground,
near Denver.

Gaston County

Hoffman Hotel, *Dallas*.
St. Joseph's Catholic Church,
McAdenville.

2 Iredell County

Ebenezer Academy, *Bethany, near
Statesville.*

Mecklenburg County

Eumenian Hall, *Davidson College*.
Mint Museum of Art, *Charlotte*.

Rowan County

Maxwell Chambers House, *Salisbury*.
St. Andrew's Episcopal Church, *near
Woodleaf.*
Setzer School, *Supplementary Educa-
tional Center, Salisbury.*

Cabarrus County

Mt. Pleasant Collegiate Institute.
Reed Gold Mine, *off N.C. #200*

Forsyth County

John Vogler House, *Old Salem,
Winston-Salem.*

Stanly County

Kron House, *Morrow Mountain State
Park.*

Rockingham County

United Methodist Church, *Wentworth*.
Wright's Tavern, *Wentworth*.

Guilford County

Blacksmith Shop, *Greensboro Historical
Museum.*
Blandwood, *Greensboro*.
Jamestown Quaker Meeting, High Point
City Park.
Mendenhall's Store, *Jamestown*.

Caswell County

County Courthouse, *Yanceyville*.
Thomas Day's Shop, *Milton*.
Warren's Store, *Prospect Hill*.

Orange County

Burwell School, *Hillsborough*.
Old County Courthouse, *Hillsborough*.
Dialectic and Philanthropic Societies,
University of North Carolina,
Chapel Hill.
Eagle Lodge, *Hillsborough*.

Chatham County

Columbus Lodge, *Pittsboro*.
Governor Manly's Law Office, *Pittsboro*.

3 Scotland County

Richmond Temperance and Literary
Society Hall, *near Wagram.*

Cumberland County

First Presbyterian Church, *Fayetteville*.
Liberty Row, *Fayetteville*.
Market House, *Fayetteville*.
Old Bluff Presbyterian Church, *near
Wade.*
Oval Ballroom, *Heritage Square,
Fayetteville.*

Harnett County

Lebanon Plantation Slave Cabin, *at
Chicora Cemetery, on N.C. #82
south of Dunn.*

Bladen County

Brown Marsh Presbyterian Church,
near Clarkton.

Wake County

Christ Episcopal Church, *Raleigh*.
State Capitol, *Raleigh*.
Dix Hill Hospital, *Raleigh*.
Mordecai House, *Mordecai Historic
Park, Raleigh.*
Peace College, *Raleigh*.

Durham County

Bennett Place, *Durham*.
Horton Grove, *Stagville Preservation
Center, northeast of Durham.*
McCown-Mangum House, *West Point
on the Eno, Durham.*
West Point Mill, *West Point on the Eno,
Durham.*

Franklin County

Laurel Mill, *near Louisburg*.

Johnston County

Harper House, *Bentonville Battle-
ground, east of U.S. #701.*

Duplin County

Liberty Hall, *Kenansville*.

Map of Historic Places

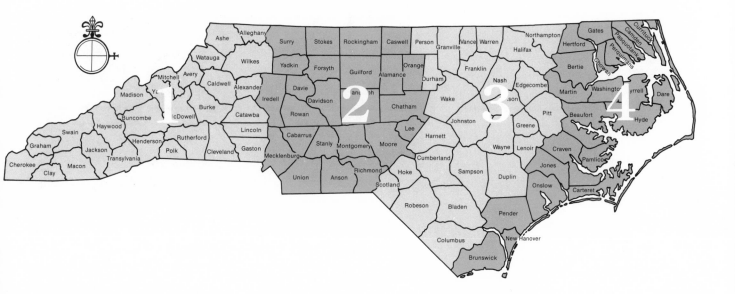

Wayne County
Governor Aycock's Birthplace, *near Fremont.*

Nash County
Stonewall Plantation, *near Rocky Mount.*
Rocky Mount Mills, Battle House, *Falls Rd., N.C. #43 and #48.*

Edgecombe County
Cotton Press, *Tarboro.*

Halifax County
Old County Clerk's Office, *Halifax.*

Northampton County
Old County Clerk's Office, *Jackson.*

4 Hertford County
Roberts-Vaughan House, *Murfreesboro.*

Martin County
Skewarkey Primitive Baptist Church, *near Williamston.*

Beaufort County
Bank of Washington.
Bonner House, *Bath.*
Zion Episcopal Church, *near Bunyan.*

New Hanover County
Fort Fisher, *south of Kure Beach.*
Zebulon Latimer House, *Wilmington.*
Thalian Hall, *Wilmington.*

Carteret County
Fort Macon, *near Atlantic Beach.*
Purvis Chapel, *Beaufort.*

Washington County
Rehoboth Methodist Church, *east of Pleasant Grove*
Somerset Place, *near Creswell.*

Hyde County
Ocracoke Lighthouse.

Dare County
Nag's Head.

Perquimans County
Bethel Baptist Church, *S.R. #1341, about five miles south of Hertford.*

Index